PRESIDENTS
AND
ARMS CONTROL

Volume II

W. Alton Jones Foundation Series
on The Presidency and Arms Control

Edited by Kenneth W. Thompson

UNIVERSITY
PRESS OF
AMERICA

Lanham • New York • London

The Miller Center

University of Virginia

Copyright © 1994 by
University Press of America®, Inc.
4720 Boston Way
Lanham, Maryland 20706

3 Henrietta Street
London WC2E 8LU England

Copublished by arrangement with
The Miller Center of Public Affairs,
University of Virginia

The views expressed by the author(s) of this publication do not necessarily represent the opinions of the Miller Center. We hold to Jefferson's dictum that: "Truth is the proper and sufficient antagonist to error, and has nothing to fear from the conflict, unless by human interposition, disarmed of her natural weapons, free argument and debate."

Library of Congress Cataloging-in-Publication Data

Presidents and arms control / edited by Kenneth W. Thompson
p. cm. — (W. Alton Jones Foundation series on the Presidency and arms
control, vol. 2)
"Copublished by arrangement with the Miller Center of Public Affairs,
University of Virginia"—T.p. verso
1. Presidents—United States. 2. Treaty-making power. 3. Arms
control—Decision making. I. Thompson, Kenneth W. II. Series.
KF5053.P74   1994   355'.033073—dc20   94-92 CIP

ISBN 0-8191-9709-2 (cloth: alk paper)
ISBN 0-8191-9710-6 (pbk: alk paper)

To Ken

whose search for
truth and justice
as the road to
self-fulfillment
is unending

Table of Contents

II. THE STORY OF AN ADMINISTRATION AND ARMS CONTROL

III. VIEWS FROM THE PRESIDENT'S NEGOTIATORS

IV. NUCLEAR WEAPONS COMPLEXITIES

Preface

For most Americans, the role of American presidents in the formulation and negotiation of arms control remains vague and unclear, and this fact provides justification for the present series of studies.

With the generous assistance of the W. Alton Jones Foundation, the Center has embarked on studies of contemporary presidents asking such questions as, How directly was a particular president involved in arms control initiatives? How much political capital was he prepared to spend in pushing forward arms control initiatives? What were his relations with his secretaries of state and defense and his negotiators? Where did arms control fall in his hierarchy of policy objectives? What contacts did he establish and maintain with foreign leaders, both of countries who were parties to the negotiation and of allies and neutral states? Who were his principal advisers?

How widely did the president cast his net in consultations with experts from the United States and abroad? Was he well prepared in terms of background and interest for arms control matters? What were his relations with Congress on arms control? How much freedom did he give negotiators to take initiatives and in what ways did he restrict their efforts? In what ways did he prepare the country for arms control initiatives and agreements? To what extent did he consult with "outsiders" as well as "insiders" in arms control? What were his most conspicuous successes and failures and how do we explain them? Did he have a special adviser in the White House or in the Departments of State or Defense on whom he depended? What kind of a balance sheet can be struck on his record in arms control?

We will pursue these questions whenever possible with former presidents, secretaries of state and defense, arms control negotiators, special assistants or advisers, analysts and scholars, and both American and foreign observers. In introductions to each study, we shall evaluate some of our findings in at least tentative terms. At the conclusion of the study, we will try to draw conclusions from the experiences of the various presidents and administrations based on our own inquiry and the studies of authorities in the field.

Introduction

The relation between presidents and arms control is not a dominant subject in much of the arms control literature. Weaponry, numbers, and negotiations are more often the focus; they are often discussed in exquisite detail.

We know, however, that the attitudes of presidents toward arms control, their willingness to expend political capital, and their skill in advancing their policies directly or through well-chosen associates and negotiators are important. A host of questions suggest themselves concerning: the president's understanding and sense of the problem; a conviction that vital and worldwide interests are involved; the ability to grasp the facts; relations with the leadership in the major executive departments, Congress, and foreign countries; a strategic sense in formulating goals and policies; the connection of arms agreements and the budget; the influence of domestic and international politics on specific agreements; choices in the negotiating process; and flexibility in response to changing circumstances and options. A president's ability to make use of negotiators in the field and key associates at home in the departments of State, Defense, and Treasury, and ACDA is also vital.

An incoming president often has much to learn from his predecessor and the team assembled for arms control initiatives. Transitions present difficult choices for both the incoming and outgoing administration. One rule of thumb concerns the need to work out guidelines upon which the respective administrations will take responsibility and for what problems. Normally, an incoming and an outgoing secretary of state will meet shortly after the election and Inauguration Day. They will undertake to sort out issues the outgoing group will handle or those that will be held for the incoming group.

If consultation and the planning of a transition is desirable for policies in general and arms control in particular, the course of some transitions makes the process difficult if not impossible. Political differences, ancient rivalries, and calculations of political gains or losses affect the willingness to cooperate. The likelihood of receiving credit or blame for the handling of particular problems enters into the equation. Even loyal public servants are not immune from the virus of politics.

Paul H. Nitze is the quintessential public servant. Because of his long career in government he has carried responsibilities in at least eight administrations out of ten that have dealt with arms control issues. In his contribution to the present volume, he goes back to the beginning of postwar arms control policy-making and evaluates the two schools of thought that emerged after the Japanese surrender. One was Bernard Brodie's definition of the atomic bomb as the "absolute weapon" making nuclear war unthinkable. The other saw atomic strategy as a necessary element of defense policy, especially as it made possible a deterrent to war. Total worldwide military disarmament and controlling such weapons were also competing views of policy.

Nitze outlines the differing arms control strategies and tactics from Truman to Bush in a *tour d'horizon* of arms control under nine presidents. He suggests certain strengths and weaknesses in particular administrations and the methods and theories used in seeking controls. Nitze goes beyond the conventional wisdom about each president and reflects on the nature of the threat. He evaluates Gulf War strategies, bomber alerts, personalizing foreign policy, the ending of the Cold War, the "walk in the woods," Reagan's massive arms buildup, the Vienna Summit, and the conduct of the Gulf War. Few American or foreign leaders can draw on a range of experience comparable to that of Ambassador Nitze.

Ambassador Ralph Earle is a former U.S. chief arms negotiator. He also served as director of the Arms Control and

Disarmament Agency (ACDA) and adviser to the president, the National Security Council, and the State Department. In his paper he addresses issues of strategy, budget, and politics in relation to arms control. He was ambassador and chief U.S. negotiator of the SALT II treaty. With the demise of the Soviet Union, the answer to the question "who is the enemy?" is more complex. As for the military budget, the question is, What can we afford and how do the costs of nuclear weapons affect security plans? Finally, he traces the effect of U.S. politics on the arms race both in restraining and advancing policies.

One of the world's authorities on arms control is Dr. Raymond Garthoff, who had major responsibility for arms control in the Kennedy, Johnson, and Nixon administrations. His contribution is a third chapter under the heading of "Presidents and Patterns in Arms Control." He writes of the arms control process and is especially attentive to the incidents in which he played an important role. He demonstrates that in some earlier administrations, disarmament and arms reductions were regarded as a form of propaganda in the Cold War. He was responsible for preparation of estimates on Soviet foreign policy and strategy in the second Eisenhower administration. These estimates helped to define those security interests that led the Soviets to favor certain measures while remaining cautious in their proposals. In the Kennedy administration, the Arms Control and Disarmament Agency was created and a new political-military staff. Garthoff discusses some of the decisions to place nuclear weapons in orbit and others that might prohibit orbital deployment of weapons of mass destruction. He analyzes space reconnaissance policy, the Limited Test Ban Treaty, unsuccessful negotiations on a comprehensive test ban treaty, nuclear site inspections, the beginnings of SALT, and Gorbachev's policies. The discussions evaluate the initiatives and responses for most of the Cold War presidents.

Don Oberdorfer is a journalist/scholar who began his career with the *Charlotte* (North Carolina) *Observer* and continued in 1960 with the *Washington Post*. His book entitled *Tet!* is the definitive work on that battle in the Vietnam War. His *The Turn: From the Cold War to a New Era* not only examines the shift from the Reagan military buildup to the pursuit of negotiations but provides substantial evidence that Reagan and Gorbachev were not the sole actors. Secretary of State George Shultz and Foreign Minister Eduard Shevardnadze were the primary negotiators who helped their leaders move from confrontation to negotiations. Three underlying factors that gave momentum to their efforts were Soviet concerns about deficits in industrial development, the country's increased urbanization, and demands for change and the need to defuse the threat of nuclear annihilation. In his chapter, Oberdorfer reviews the background of his classic study and his conclusions concerning the role of the four leaders: Gorbachev, Reagan, and their foreign secretaries. The Washington journalist not only reports what each contributed to improved relations but some of the psychological, political, and philosophical reasons that led each of them to act as they did.

Ambassador Maynard Glitman had held a series of major appointments in arms negotiation including deputy chief of the U.S. delegation in the Intermediate Nuclear Force (INF) negotiations from 1981-1984 and ambassador and chief negotiator in INF negotiations in Geneva from 1985-88. Among the topics Glitman considers in his chapter are the organization of the government for arms control policy-making in the Reagan administration and the turf battles that kept ACDA somewhat in the background. By contrast, negotiators in the field had a major impact on strategy, tactics, and implementation, as did the secretary of state, who enabled the negotiators to raise the ante. On major issues, the secretary's participation is essential. The National Security Council helped move the bureaucracy and supported negotiators and their tactics. Paul Nitze, who was head of the delegation for two years, and Glitman, his deputy for two years before succeeding Nitze, saw eye-to-eye. Glitman considered that there wouldn't have been an INF Treaty without President Reagan. Flexibility was his hallmark. The Glitman paper is a masterpiece in the explanation of governance and policy-making and the cooperation of the many parties to an American approach to arms control.

In his second presentation, Ambassador Earle approaches U.S. policy toward arms control. He is a former director of ACDA and a chief negotiator on SALT II. In a wide-ranging but well-informed essay he identifies widespread myths on arms control. He questions whether Carter's human rights crusade delayed an arms agreement with the Soviets. In a carefully worded analysis, he surveys the role of successive presidents on arms control. Earle is critical of the delay in arms agreements that results from transitions. Finally, he analyzes the costs of the buildup of nuclear weapons and donations by so-called little countries that contributed small amounts. Earle's vast experience is crucial to the building of site selection.

The Washington Conference, 1921-22, is an example of the interrelation of a president, his secretary of state, and Senate leaders in arms negotiations. Professor Thomas Buckley draws on his classic study on the subject in a chapter that illustrates the interplay of two of the main branches of government and the public. Buckley sketches in and evaluates the main elements of the treaty and their effect on the participating nations. The Four-Power Pacific Treaty involving the United States, Great Britain, France, and Japan was the subject of a ratification struggle in the Senate in which the senior senator, Henry Cabot Lodge, was the key figure. Lodge was the head of the Republican party, and his chief ally was a Democrat, Senator Oscar W. Underwood. Secretary of State Charles Evans Hughes was a leading player. The president was Warren G. Harding and the success of the treaty was Harding's single most important accomplishment.

George Perkovich reaches beyond national boundaries in a challenging discussion of "Nuclear Weapons Complexes in the Post-Cold War World." He asks what can be done to deal with the breakdown in the "physical and intellectual infrastructures of nuclear weapons complexes." He points to three areas of urgent concern: the management of the costly and environment-threatening dismantling of nuclear weapons complexes; the instability brought about by change of ownership of nuclear weapons; and the possibility of unemployed scientists and engineers from the Soviet Union and Eastern Europe being recruited by nations seeking nuclear weapons. Perkovich considers possible remedies to each of these problems. For example, he explores the possibility of alternative career paths for nuclear personnel. He goes beyond proposals for dealing with particular problems and observes that any grand strategy would require world leaders to give the highest priority to seeking new avenues for the prevention of nuclear war.

Based on the Acheson-Lilienthal proposals a half century ago, he suggests the need for an international regime to control nuclear weapons. In the bulk of his chapter, he examines the requirements, justification, and possibilities for such a regime.

I.

PRESIDENTS AND PATTERNS
IN
ARMS CONTROL

CHAPTER ONE

Presidents and Arms Control: Reviewing the Facts[*]

PAUL NITZE

NARRATOR: James Reston wrote, "The problem in Washington is not people who seek power, but those who shun and avoid the responsible exercise of power. Paul Nitze and a handful of American leaders, including Harry S Truman, are exceptions." The best way of footnoting that statement is to remind ourselves that Paul Nitze's career is a chronicle of the responsible exercise of power.

He was vice president of Dillon and Reed, president of P. H. Nitze Investment Company, and then along with James Forrestal and others, he left Wall Street and went to Washington to take up responsibilities in the government. He was vice chairman of the Strategic Bombing Survey, deputy director of the Office of International Trade and director of the Policy Planning staff in the State Department. He returned to the private sector and founded the School for Advanced International Studies with Secretary of State Christian Herter and others. He occupied that very important post in the Defense Department, assistant secretary for

---

[*]*Presented in a Forum at the Miller Center of Public Affairs on 1 October 1991.*

international security affairs, and then became secretary of the Navy.

He was deputy secretary of defense and a member of the U.S. Strategic Arms Limitation Talks (SALT) delegation. He was head of the U.S. negotiating team for the arms control talks in Geneva from 1981 until 1984. He was special adviser to President Reagan and Secretary Shultz for arms control in the last stages of that administration.

He has received many honors, including the U.S. Medal of Freedom, the George Marshall Award, and the Order of the Merit of the Federal Republic of Germany. We are proud to say he has also received the Burkett Miller prize.

His responsible exercise of power has extended to the field of education. In a few days he will receive the Thayer Award at West Point. He has lectured at the Kennan Institute and the International Institute of Strategic Studies in Zurich. He is returning in a few days to Saint Gallens in Switzerland to lecture on issues and problems in the field of politics. His interest in the responsible exercise of power and education has been evident through a long and distinguished career. We feel highly privileged that Paul Nitze would talk to us on the topic "Presidents and Arms Control: Reviewing the Facts."

MR. NITZE: The task that Kenneth has set for me is a daunting one. I believe there are ten presidents who have worked with arms control issues, and I find it difficult to sort out which ones did what, what their attitudes were, and how they addressed the problem.

Arms control became a serious U.S. policy issue only after the use of the first two nuclear weapons at Hiroshima and Nagasaki. They provided the Japanese emperor and his advisers with an excuse to override the military and accept the surrender terms. Therefore, they demonstrated the potential overwhelming importance of nuclear weapons in the world.

Two schools of thought arose in the United States immediately after the Japanese surrender. One of them was led by a man named Bernard Brodie, who was with the RAND Corporation. His view was that the very existence of nuclear weapons made war impossible for the future. His view was widely accepted around the world and in the United States at the time.

The opposing view was in effect spearheaded by those of us who had done the actual measurements at Hiroshima and Nagasaki as part of the mandate given us by the President for the USSBS (the U.S. Strategic Bombing Survey). We were told to measure in detail all the effects of the nuclear weapons as actually used and to extrapolate from that recommendations for the organization of the Defense Department and the main defense policy issues in the future. It was our view, which was different from that of Bernard Brodie, that we had to take this development extremely seriously in our defense policy and see what needed to be done to mitigate the possible future dangers to the United States, its friends, and its allies. We thought we had to figure out how to minimize dangers, mitigate problems, and survive in a world in which such weapons were possible.

Both schools could agree that we should try to negotiate controls over such weapons, and that led to the overwhelming consensus that we should try to get these weapons under international control. This consensus led to the Acheson-Lilienthal report, the Baruch plan, and negotiations with the Soviets on some method under the aegis of the United Nations to get these weapons and the raw materials thereof under international control. There have been long arguments as to whether we did it right, whether the Baruch plan wasn't going backward rather than forward, and whether we gave the Russians a real chance to join with us in that effort.

I believe we did give them a real chance. The problem really was a different one: namely, their intelligence network had been closely following what we were doing. They knew all about the Manhattan Project. They had decided earlier to build nuclear weapons of their own. They were well along on that project, and they wanted to delay things until they could talk to us on equal terms in the nuclear field. As a result, the Soviets did turn down all U.S.-proposed plans, and instead they concentrated on a propaganda approach. That was centered on the Swedish peace appeal. The Soviets promoted the slogan of "total and complete disarmament," I believe, as a cover for their intense program to catch up in the nuclear field.

During this period U.S. policy toward nuclear weapons was more in the hands of the Congress, particularly the Joint Atomic Energy Committee, than in the hands of the executive branch.

There was a basic disagreement between those who believed passionately in the slogan of "total military disarmament worldwide" and many of the more prudent people in the Pentagon and elsewhere who believed in jointly agreed international measures negotiated under a U.N. aegis to control such armaments, not to abolish them. In the executive branch the subject was turned over to the U.N. division of the State Department. Bernard Bechhoefer was head of that organization, and he had a point of view that was common in the United States at that time: that everything had to be done with complete U.N. control, and that all things were good in the context of world government under the United Nations.

But he had no real sense at all, I thought, of how you got from here to there, and the task of doing something about arms control was taken over by Bob Tufts and Bob Ferguson in the Policy Planning staff. During that period, we were talking a lot, but nothing concrete towards arms control really got done. At the outset of the Eisenhower administration, primary attention turned to reducing the enormous cost of defense by concentrating on deterrence through the threat of using nuclear weapons at times and places of our choosing, as it was phrased. We used the threat of nuclear weapons against the Soviet military and civilian installations in cities to deter any aggressive Soviet acts. It was a money-saving scheme and set us back, I thought, during the entire period of the Eisenhower administration. I can't think of any really constructive work on arms control that was done during the Eisenhower administration. I may be wrong.

The Eisenhower administration did create the Gaither Committee, which concentrated on reducing the vulnerability of the principle elements of our deterrent forces to surprise attack. At one time, Walt Rostow worked for them and suggested an open skies proposal, but that could obviously have little appeal to as secretive a society as the U.S.S.R.

6

Most of the pressure for arms control negotiations at that time came from private organizations and organizations and committees associated with the United Nations. The principal focus of that pressure became to reduce worldwide fallout from atmospheric tests of thermonuclear weapons.

When John Foster Dulles died and Christian Herter took over as secretary of state, Chris gave arms control higher priority and asked Fred Eaton to become head of the U.S. team in the eight-nation disarmament talks in Geneva. For a long time the Soviets made enormous progress propaganda-wise with their slogan of "complete and total disarmament," while we were talking about interim measures. That didn't have any propaganda oomph!

Finally, we decided to change our slogan to "phased complete and total disarmament." The Soviets were so mad at us for taking the heart of their propaganda slogan and converting it to our use that they walked out of the negotiations, which was the end of the eight-nation disarmament negotiations. But it was a triumph in the propaganda sense. The Soviets lost the basis for what they had been working for.

After President Kennedy was elected in 1960, he was determined to make arms control a central facet of his program. He and McNamara asked me to head ISA (International Security Affairs), to which Kennedy had referred arms control problems. McNamara asked me specifically to put arms control at the top of my agenda, but there were too many other things that we had to deal with in ISA at the time for me to initially give that subject much attention.

Jock McCloy had been backstopping the U.S. team participating in the eight-nation disarmament negotiations in Geneva and also in the discussions regarding the resumption of work in the U.N. Committee on Disarmament. The key point under debate was the composition of the group to control the third stage of mutual reduction of nuclear weapons leading to total disarmament.

It had been agreed that a troika, with one member appointed by the United States and one by the Soviet Union, should be custodian of the last remaining nuclear weapons. The question was how the third member of that troika should be appointed. The

U.S.S.R. was adamant that it have the right to veto any candidate. We were likewise concerned that the third member be someone satisfactory to the West, and specifically to the United States.

When Mr. Kennedy went to Vienna in June 1961 for discussions with Mr. Khrushchev, the main talks were directly between the two principals, each with his own interpreters. The rest of us on both sides waited in an adjacent room in case either of the principals wished to consult with a member of his team. Neither did, so the Soviet advisers and we Americans had nothing to do but talk to each other.

The main subject of our conversation was how to resolve this issue of the third man of the troika. We made no progress, even though we discussed it hour after hour. It was inherently insoluble. The distrust between the two sides was too great.

It was only after a number of nuclear-testing moratoria and surprise violations thereof by the Soviets that it became possible to lay the foundations for a mutually acceptable limited test ban treaty. Two factors were at work. The first was that the Soviets had carried out such a complete series of atmospheric tests that there was little to be learned from further such tests. Underground tests were adequate to satisfy the requirements for ascertaining the reliability of the nuclear trigger mechanisms.

The other factor was that the worldwide spread of fallout from the atmospheric testing of thermonuclear weapons, particularly the mammoth, 60-megaton Soviet devices, was so obviously a threat to the population of the entire northern hemisphere that continued testing would have been a political liability to whichever side were to continue it.

Once this was understood on both sides, it was no great problem to negotiate the limited test ban treaty. When we in Washington had worked out the provisions that we were prepared to accept, I think it took Averell Harriman only two weeks in Moscow to work the treaty out with the Soviets. It was a cinch, once you correctly worked out the essential elements.

During the last days of the Kennedy administration, some of us working for McNamara came to the conclusion that multilateral negotiations under the aegis of the United Nations were bound to be dominated by East-West propaganda considerations, and were unlikely to be effective in achieving useful, stabilizing reductions between the United States and the U.S.S.R. It appeared to us that bilateral negotiations between the United States and the U.S.S.R. would be more likely to produce positive results. Just before Mr. Kennedy's assassination, McNamara became convinced of the soundness of our recommendations. He raised those ideas with President Johnson early in his incumbency, and Tommy Thompson, who was our ambassador in Moscow, took them up with the Soviet leaders but received a cool reaction. They were raised again at the 1967 Glassboro summit meeting between Johnson and Kosygin, and eventually the Soviets agreed that such negotiations, in their phrase, "might be possible." A date was set for the negotiators to meet, but the negotiations were made politically impossible by the Soviet invasion of Czechoslovakia in 1968. Johnson hoped to revive them before he left office, but he was unsuccessful.

Nixon understood the political importance of promptly getting into active arms control negotiations. He understood that right away. He was a very intelligent man, I thought. (He had other difficulties.) He relied upon Kissinger for his staff work and advice, but kept overall guidance in his own hands.

The two of them adopted a two-track negotiation procedure. Gerard Smith was made head of the U.S. arms control delegation with the formal and overt responsibility to conduct the negotiations. But Nixon and Kissinger reserved for themselves a special, higher, direct channel of negotiations with Brezhnev and Dobrynin.

There was constant friction within the U.S. side, not only within the delegation—which had representatives from each one of the major agencies involved in the negotiations—but also between the delegation and the White House. The negotiations did produce the ABM Treaty, which despite its ambiguities, I considered and still consider to be a worthwhile agreement. There was also a so-called interim agreement on offensive weapons, which then and now I consider to have been worthless. Those two documents were ratified by the Senate in 1972. By 1974 the arms control process had become corrupted by Nixon's need to use it to demonstrate his indispensability in negotiations with the Soviets as a defense against the growing pressure for his impeachment.

In order to claim progress in arms control, Nixon entered into the Moscow Agreement with Brezhnev, which I considered to be worse than useless. It was to expire within ten years and eliminated the possibility of a worthwhile treaty limiting offensive weapons in a manner comparable to the limitations on defensive weapons that were of indefinite duration in the ABM Treaty.

When Ford succeeded to the presidency after Nixon resigned to avoid impeachment, his principal task was to restore confidence in the executive branch. I thought he did so with solid common sense and good judgment. His principal adviser on national security, defense, and arms control issues was Donald Rumsfeld, of whom I thought extremely highly. Serious negotiations on arms control, however, would have to await the outcome of the next election.

Mr. Carter's role in arms control was ambiguous, and to me, is still difficult to understand fully. During the early portion of his campaign for the Democratic nomination, he announced to the press that I was his principal adviser on national security and defense issues. Within days it became clear that this was not the full story. He had many advisers, including Rosalynn, his wife. She seemed seriously to believe that she and her husband received direct guidance from the Almighty! After a while it turned out that Cyrus Vance, Paul Warnke, Harold Brown, and Stuart Eizenstat had much greater influence with Carter than I did. I was asked by Tony Lake, who was then his principal adviser on NSC matters, to prepare a paper for Carter on how to handle the arms control problems, which I did.

A few years later I had lunch with the Finnish ambassador to the United States. He had just returned from Plains, Georgia, where he had called on ex-President Carter. The ambassador said that Carter, who was going through his papers, had before him the paper on arms control that I had prepared. He further said that Carter commented that he might have done better if he had taken its recommendation seriously. I have no idea if that actually happened, but that is what the Finnish ambassador told me. In any case, the way in which the arms control negotiations were handled by Carter and Vance seemed to me to leave much to be desired.

Paul Nitze

When Reagan took office, the first study of what the new arms control position of the United States should be was organized by Mike May and the staff of the Lawrence Livermore National Laboratory, and Ralph Earle, the outgoing head of the Arms Control and Disarmament Agency.

The first concrete arms control decisions that Reagan had to make sprang from pressure from our European allies caused by the rapid Soviet deployment beginning in 1979 of the SS-20 medium-range, MIRVed nuclear mobile missiles. These missiles presented a direct threat to every important target in Europe, the Middle East, South Asia, and the Far East.

Our European partners, led by Helmut Schmidt, demanded that the United States take measures to offset the SS-20 threat, which led to the two-track decision. The United States would be asked to create and prepare to deploy in Europe the cruise and Pershing II missiles, and concurrently to enter into negotiations with the Soviets for the elimination of all medium-range nuclear missiles on both sides. This so-called zero option was supported by Richard Perle and me, and was fought by Richard Burt. The resulting situation was called the "battle of the two Richards."

President Reagan finally decided with enthusiasm for the zero option. The negotiations took place in Geneva and resulted in the "walk in the woods," and the final Soviet walkout from the negotiations in November 1982. Productive negotiations did not resume until Mr. Gorbachev had become general secretary of the Politburo. From that point on the story has become dominated by the internal collapse of the Warsaw Pact and of the Communist party structure, and by the dissolution of the Soviet Union itself. The continuing negotiations centered on arms control but gradually expanded to cover the entire range of East-West relations. They were at the heart of the political developments of those years.

The guiding force on the U.S. side came in part from President Reagan and in part from George Shultz. The President had two deep convictions. The first was that over the years, world public opinion would not tolerate the continued threat of mutual nuclear destruction as the cornerstone of the maintenance of peace. Politically, he thought it was necessary for the United States to aspire to making nuclear weapons obsolete, which could come about by mutual elimination of nuclear weapons or by defenses that were sufficiently effective to make them obsolete.

The second of Mr. Reagan's convictions was that the United States system of government—checks and balances between three independent branches of government and an economy largely dependent upon a free-market system—was, without any doubt, superior to an evil, totalitarian empire with a centrally directed economy such as that in the Soviet Union.

Shultz understood and basically agreed with President Reagan's conviction, but was much more sensitive to the necessary processes of moving step-by-step from where we were to where we wanted to get. It was a pleasure to work under their joint guidance. Shultz always encouraged those working for him to take the initiative boldly. He would back you up when you got into trouble. He would try to keep you informed of what was going on in the battles of the President's mind. Some battles he won, some he lost, but overall it was a great success.

When Bush took office in 1989, he considered his principle task to unify the Republican party by bringing its right wing back into the fold. This meant cutting all ties with Shultz, who was considered too middle-of-the-road by the Republican right. As a result, Shultz and his policies were anathema to the Bush administration. Arms control, I believe, has *followed* the 1989 revolution in Central Europe and 1991 revolution in the Soviet Union, rather than contributing to them, as many believe.

Let me summarize my thoughts on the roles of various presidents on arms control: Truman, backed by Acheson and Marshall, was responsible for the creation of the basic U.S. postwar policy represented by containment, NSC-68, NATO, and the Marshall Plan. He was not himself active in arms control policy. Eisenhower's regime was, in my mind, a negative period for arms control.

I thought Kennedy was an indifferent leader on arms control. Initially he made the right moves, but the times weren't ripe for him to do much beyond the limited test ban. McNamara and his staff were far more prescient and forward-thinking on arms control matters than Mr. Kennedy or his NSC staff. At least that was my impression of it.

12

Johnson seemed to me to be the first president who fully grasped that world sentiment about arms control constituted a force that had to be reckoned with, both externally and domestically. Nixon also recognized the importance of this new political reality, but he had the misfortune to have Kissinger as his principal adviser and he had to contend with Watergate—two great handicaps.

Ford had no chance to do anything on arms control, and Carter got himself off track early, suffered from conflicting advice, and was bewildered by the hostage crisis and the Soviet invasion of Afghanistan. So that leaves us with the presidents we know very well, Mr. Reagan and Mr. Bush. That is a summary of my tale.

QUESTION: What about President Bush's speech of Friday, 27 September 1991?

MR. NITZE: I was of two minds about the President's speech. In the first place, some of the things that he advocated I thought were belated. They should have been done earlier, particularly the provisions with respect to eliminating sea-based tactical nuclear weapons. I had been fighting for that for a long period of time, but received no support.

I thought other parts of the speech were more directed to the propaganda mode that had been dominant in the early days of arms control. It seemed to me that the speech was addressed to the political hopes and needs of the moment, rather than to building a long-range, solidly thought-through program. He was using many of the things that had already been decided on, such as getting rid of the remaining tactical nuclear weapons, short-range nuclear weapons in Europe and getting START ratified and moving on from START. Those things I thought had been worked out in advance.

The thing that worried me was his decision to take our bombers off alert. I can't imagine a more stupid thing myself! Until the other side gets rid of its nuclear weapons, deterrence is important, particularly against the danger of a surprise attack. I don't think it's right to increase the risk and temptation to somebody suddenly getting hold of the nuclear arsenal and saying, "You've left a great opportunity."

The one thing that would destroy the United States is the Soviet strategic long-range nuclear arsenal, their SS-18s and SS-19s. They are the only things that could defeat the United States in a surprise attack. We should not take any chances with that.

Bush didn't address the problem of testing, but certainly the Russians are going to raise that. As long as we rely upon our nuclear arsenal for deterrence, we ought to be sure that the weapons work as they are intended. We should continue testing until the Soviet threat has diminished materially from what it has been. I don't believe it has yet diminished. They are continuing to build more long-range nuclear missiles in number than we are. In those circumstances I think it would be improvident to move too fast.

NARRATOR: Is the media partly responsible for what you referred to as a propaganda effort? I understood that the administration did not intend to make a presidential speech, but the media got advance notice of the proposal and encouraged, almost demanded, that there be a presidential address.

MR. NITZE: I don't know. I'm not part of the administration any more. You may be right, but I think they were playing with awfully short deadlines in this thing. They informed the Russians one day before the announcement was made. It is very hard to keep these things secret for long. They are bound to leak.

NARRATOR: Since we are in this area, would you mind discussing the limited-information and short-notice decisions that a president has to make, and the need to change his mind if new facts enter into the picture?

MR. NITZE: When I was in Switzerland I found myself emphasizing one particular point, which I think many of the other people at the conference thought might be important: If you want to compete successfully in this big game of national security with its great dangers, you have to move fast. When something happens that requires action, you have to move right away. You can't delay. You have to act on imperfect information. The President did act within minutes—upon imperfect information—the moment Saddam Hussein crossed the border into Kuwait. You can't wait to get checks and double checks on accuracy of the information; you have to act.

One thing is crystal clear: With the passage of time you will have better information. If that better information contradicts the information you originally had, then you have to change your mind. It is that process of changing your mind the moment you have better information that is the most difficult thing for leaders to do consistently. If you don't do it in time, you are bound to let errors get bigger and they are harder to correct thereafter.

In the Gulf War, I thought one example of that was when the President directed General Schwarzkopf not to advance more deeply into Iraq, even though there was nothing between him and Baghdad. One can understand why Bush made that decision; he thought that the Republican Guards would murder Saddam Hussein and it would be better for them to be responsible for it. Beyond that, Bush thought it would be better for him not to take responsibility for the internal conflicts and difficulties between the nationalities and sects in Iraq.

We could understand that initial decision as probably right and wise, but within five days it was clear that the Republican Guards were not going to murder Saddam Hussein. The black shirts who were working directly for Saddam Hussein knew that they had no future without him in command and had demonstrated they were strong enough to prevent Republican Guard actions. So after five days, Bush should have changed his order and released General Schwarzkopf to go north. If he had gone north at that time, I think he would have been met with open arms by almost everybody there. He would have had to go up with sufficient force to make it clear that he could overwhelm all these black shirts, which was easy to do at the time.

It would have been a different world if we could have separated Saddam Hussein from Iraq. I don't know who would have taken his place, but the result couldn't have been worse. I think the situation in the Middle East would have been measurably better had that been done.

QUESTION: If you have serious reservations about the program announced by President Bush last Friday, what would you suggest that he do instead now in the field of arms control?

MR. NITZE: I would not take our bombers off alert. Most of the other things I would be for, but it was the presentation that bothered me. It was in the form of a propaganda speech. It didn't give an honest account as to how all these actions he announced came about. I think many of them were already in the bag; cessation of the program for the rail mobile missile system had already been decided by the Congress.

I think many of the things which he takes credit for were not in the realm of the possible when the speech was made. I have an awkward inhibition, which is that I think you do better if you stick to the truth.

QUESTION: One columnist speculated that Bush stopped short of Baghdad because Gorbachev had sent word to him that if the United States or the coalition went to Baghdad, Gorbachev would be overthrown.

MR. NITZE: I hadn't heard that, but let's assume for a minute that there was some such risk. An error that is often made by people, particularly in the United States, is to associate foreign policy issues with individuals.

We used to associate China policy with whether you loved Chiang Kai-shek. The whole argument was whether you loved him enough. The same problem arose with Iran over whether you loved the shah enough. But nobody looked upon the Iranian issue in terms of the country itself. They looked upon it as shah or anti-shah.

You can think of many instances in which we have made this mis-association of an individual with a much larger issue. I think we have done the same thing with Gorbachev, and I think the executive branch in particular has done this with Gorbachev. They have associated his survival as being the essence of policy toward the former U.S.S.R. I think this has been a grave error. I think Mr. Gorbachev speaks truth when he says, "I am a true and dedicated

16

believer in Marxist-Leninism and the eventual triumph of socialism worldwide." When he says "socialism," he means it in the Soviet context. I think he means that and has meant it.

Yeltsin now says that Gorbachev no longer means what he said in the past. Maybe Yeltsin is right; I don't know, but it certainly was true in the past. I think Gorbachev was saying these things because he really meant them. But this idea of deviating from what we think ought to be the policy just because somebody says it is going to hurt Gorbachev is ridiculous.

QUESTION: As one of the architects of the containment doctrine, did you ever think you would live long enough to see the conclusion of it? Has it turned out as well as you might have expected?

MR. NITZE: George Kennan and I used to argue somewhat about how long it would take to be effective. It was George's idea that it might take 15 years to contain Soviet expansionism. It was my view that it might take as long as 15 to 30 years. Obviously, we were both wrong. It took almost 50 years.

As to the second part of your question on whether containment has turned out as effectively as George and I thought it would, George made this very clear. Once a period of time had gone by and their leaders began to look inward, then Soviet communism would radically fall apart. They would see the damage done to Russian institutions and character, the immense cost of competing in this broad field, the enormous physical and cultural sacrifices, and once they began the process of reform, then the whole thing would radically fall apart. And that has happened!

You couldn't foresee exactly how it would happen. If the Soviet Union began to fall apart, you couldn't tell which part would fall apart first: the ethnic part, the economic part, the cultural part, or the survival of the party. The idea that it would fall apart once they began the process of reform was clear and has turned out to be true.

QUESTION: Why wasn't the "walk in the woods" followed up more closely? Do you think that was a political decision then or was it taken too abruptly?

MR. NITZE: The ideas that I proposed to Yuli Kvitsinsky in the "walk in the woods" had not been cleared in Washington. Yuli and I put them forward as an exploration to see if he and I could develop some ideas for us to submit to our two governments with no obligation on the part of either. Those ideas had not been approved by either government. You can't explore new unapproved ideas if you think there is going to be a leak, so it was kept secret on both sides, and I think properly so.

It became clear within a week after the "walk in the woods" that Kvitsinsky hadn't gotten any useful support for it in his own government. I didn't get overwhelming support in our government either. It was a good attempt, but I thought it would be wrong to make it known to Helmut Schmidt. Eugene Rostow, who in a way was my boss at the time, did try to tell Helmut Schmidt about this thing. He thought it was so important that our allies know about it that he tried to tell the British, the Germans, and—I think—the Italians, but he was bounced for that, and properly so. Such a leak wasn't his decision to make; it was a decision for higher authority.

QUESTION: Reagan based his massive military buildup in the early 1980s in part on the stated need to negotiate from a position of strength, but the consequence of that has been the burden of a horrendous national debt. Do you think it was worth it?

MR. NITZE: I do indeed, because I don't think the two things are necessarily related. Going forward with a vigorous defense program should be accompanied by an increase in taxes and an announcement to the country that we have to pay for this as we go. So if our fiscal policies had been commensurate with what we were doing in the defense field, we would have had a better chance.

That was true all along when we wrote NSC-68. At that time we recommended that taxes be increased and that controls be put on raw materials, to see that the economy was protected from the expansion in our defense program that we were recommending. If you keep the two things together, you have a chance of coming through. If you raise expenditures but do nothing about the revenue side, you are bound to run into inflation.

QUESTION: Given your history with all the postwar presidents, could you comment on whether arms control now has too great an importance in foreign affairs?

MR. NITZE: As my long tale illustrates, I don't think presidents had much to do with arms control in the earlier years. This only became an important matter with Presidents Johnson and Nixon, and even they didn't do it very well. So, whether you should select a president on the basis of what he does about arms control is dubious.

It would seem to me that if a president doesn't realize that arms control is an important matter in both international and domestic politics, he is living in a different world than the one I know. It is very important for a president to be familiar with this issue. I think all presidents since Johnson have realized that this is an important factor.

QUESTION: You have expressed some misgivings concerning the wisdom of the administration in canceling the strategic bomber alert at this stage. Is your suspicion based upon your experience in dealings with Russians or do you have some specific insight into what has happened? You indicated that you were no longer part of this administration, which I assume means that you don't have the benefit of the intelligence that is available to the administration. Would having access to that affect your decision?

MR. NITZE: Frankly, I don't have much concern about not having access to all the information, because having had access to it for 40 or 50 years and still working with people who have access to it, I don't believe that this information is much different than what the public has access to. I think people make much too much of so-called classified information's bearing upon the essentials of public policy.

As to the first part of your question, I don't believe my experience would give me any particular insight into it. My approach is more general. That is, we have all seen that surprising things happen, and when things are uncertain, you should be careful.

People talk about excessively pessimistic evaluations, but one should look back at the evaluations made before World War I and World War II. What actually happened at Pearl Harbor was much worse than anybody imagined, so that the idea you can have too pessimistic an assumption is generally false. Things are uncertain, opponents have always attempted to capitalize on surprise, and you want to be prepared against the ultimate risks, even though you don't see anything in the immediate offing.

I don't believe that there is anything in the immediate offing, but the question remains valid as to whether taking our forces off alert might decrease the risks and increase the benefits to a foreign power that might decide to try a surprise attack upon the United States. I think to invite that sort of thing by improvidence in our standard operating procedures is a mistake. I wouldn't do it.

QUESTION: Going back to Vienna in 1961, do you recall what actions President Kennedy took and how he got along with Khrushchev? What were the results of the conference?

MR. NITZE: After these meetings between the President and Mr. Khrushchev, Chip Bohlen, our interpreter, would dictate his notes as to what had gone on verbatim, word by word, during the interchanges with Khrushchev. We wouldn't get access to those transcripts of what had gone on until about 10 o'clock in the evening.

I can remember my reaction after reading the transcript of the first day's conversations. I was shocked that the President did not stand up for himself or for the United States at all. He seemed to be shy and overwhelmed by the force and vigor of Khrushchev's denunciation and humiliation of him. Khrushchev had a will to demonstrate that he was the strong man, that he had lived through the tough infighting you had to go through to rise to the top in the Communist party.

Kennedy was a rich man's son. He had had no experience in this kind of thing and was unworthy to be Khrushchev's opposite number. The first day was a disaster. Kennedy floundered around and was unable to defend himself. During the course of the night, however, he gathered together his resources and the next day he did a much better job, dealing with Khrushchev with distinction.

QUESTION: What will be the effect on arms control if we merely take the warhead material from the systems we are destroying and put them into new systems like the Trident D5 missile or the single-warhead intercontinental ballistic missile that Bush proposed in his Friday's speech?

MR. NITZE: I think there is enough nuclear material already, so we can have enough warheads for the maximum forces that we intend to deploy. We are not going to have as many nuclear weapons or delivery systems as we have had in the past. Whereas for many years we have been devoting about 6.5 to 7 percent of our gross national product to defense, I think in the future it will decline to 3.5 percent or less. So we are going to reduce the share of our economy devoted defense by about half. We are not going to have the resources to do as much as we have been doing. We're going to have fewer weapons, less support for those weapons, smaller military forces in the future, and that is given.

There exists plenty of nuclear material for the nuclear weapons that would be needed for that smaller force. In any case, nuclear weapons are a minuscule part of our whole defense establishment. Twelve percent of defense costs go into strategic, nuclear, or atomic systems, and only a tenth of that goes into the nuclear weapons involved. Thus, 1 to 2 percent of our defense expenditures go into nuclear weapons.

QUESTION: What are your views on the minimum number of secured weapons it would take to deter the Soviets? Also, what is wrong with stopping nuclear testing on the same day the Soviets stopped?

MR. NITZE: With respect to the first question, there is some argument between all of us in this field as to the minimum number that it would be wise to have, and this depends in part upon whether one is taking into account the fact that there are other countries besides the U.S.S.R. and the United States that have

21

nuclear weapons. I don't think one should ignore that at this stage, because it is so much easier to negotiate with the Russians alone than it would be to negotiate with the Russians, British, French, Chinese, Israelis, and everybody else at the same time. The number of problems goes up exponentially when one increases the number of participants in a negotiation. So at this stage, I would think we should stick to U.S.-U.S.S.R. negotiations and not get above a number where the nth country problems become too important. The situation would be stable between the two of us even though the British, French, Chinese, and Israelis go ahead with their current programs.

I think that the number under those circumstances should be not less than 3,000 to 5,000 on the Soviet side and on our side. Then it would depend upon what the rules are under which each side would be permitted to deploy their 5,000 weapons. I think it is important that those rules make the possession of destabilizing weapons like the large MIRVed-based systems illegal, which is what the President has also been talking about. You could go through those rules and design something that would be much safer and much more stable with 5,000 on both sides rather than higher numbers. That would be a much bigger cut than anything else proposed by the President's speech or anything else we have been talking about so far.

With regard to your second question, as long as we rely on nuclear weapons as the bottom line of our security—which I think we are going to do for the indefinite future until the Soviets get way down below where they are now, much lower even than 5,000—then I think we should be sure that those weapons are reliable and work the way they are intended. To be sure of that, you have to continue some testing, and I don't see why we shouldn't continue it. I am all for continuing underground testing as long as it is the type of testing that is necessary to preserve our confidence in the reliability and utility of those weapons we do have.

QUESTION: I would like to go back for a minute to the point you made about the president being able to change his mind. You indicated that all or most of these decisions had to be made immediately. Why is it that some of these decisions can't be delayed until further information is available? I dare say if the response at the outset of the Vietnam situation had been delayed, it might have been a different decision.

MR. NITZE: I believe it would have been a great mistake on the part of President Bush if he had delayed the decision to authorize General Schwarzkopf to take command of our forces in the Persian Gulf and to begin to work to throw back this invasion of Kuwait. If he had delayed a day, the risks would have been much greater, and Saddam Hussein might then have gone down to occupy Saudi Arabia. We could have gotten him out of Saudi Arabia eventually, but it would have been a much longer, more dangerous, dubious enterprise than it actually turned out to be.

I repeat: There are occasions when you take enormous risks if you delay at all. It depends on the situation. There are some situations where you have plenty of time and it doesn't require an immediate decision, and then it is wise to take as much time as is available. But you should always be prepared to make decisions immediately if that is what the situation requires.

You were suggesting that we might have been better off in Vietnam if we had taken more time to decide. My recollection is that we took lots of time. It took years before we finally got ourselves thoroughly embroiled in Vietnam.

COMMENT: I was thinking about the Gulf of Tonkin.

MR. NITZE: There I think your point is well taken. We might have taken longer before reacting in that instance, but the evidence that we relied upon was intercepts of messages sent by the destroyers to their headquarters that they had sunk a U.S. destroyer.

We argued that out with Bill Fulbright! He said it was nonsensical to take those intercepts seriously because we knew the destroyer hadn't been sunk, but on the other hand, we knew that they had sent this message back, claiming that they had sunk it. Whether that was a wise decision or not will remain controversial for a long time. I thought that having gotten these intercepts, the decision to act was proper, but maybe that was wrong.

NARRATOR: The School of Advanced International Studies, now the Nitze School, and the American Foreign Policy Research Center have made a unique contribution to understanding. They are the long shadow of a single individual. Because of these institutions, the hard thinking that Mr. Nitze has devoted to foreign policy is likely to go on for decades to come. We are extremely grateful and thank him very much.

CHAPTER TWO

Presidents and Arms Control: Strategy, Budgets, and Politics[*]

AMBASSADOR RALPH EARLE

NARRATOR: Ambassador Ralph Earle is former director of the Arms Control and Disarmament Agency (ACDA). In this capacity, he served as adviser to the president, the National Security Council, and the State Department across the discipline of arms control and disarmament. From 1978 to 1980 he was chief U.S. negotiator, with the rank of ambassador, of the SALT II Treaty. Earlier still, he was ACDA's representative on the U.S. SALT delegation. He was an officer in the U.S. Army Corps of Engineers and Counter Intelligence Corps.

Ambassador Earle is a graduate of Harvard College and Harvard Law School, and has practiced law as a partner of Morgan, Lewis & Bokius in Philadelphia, and Baker & Daniels in Washington. Currently, he is chairman of the board of directors of the Lawyers' Alliance for World Security, and executive council member of the Committee for National Security.

We are happy that Ambassador Earle could join us for this discussion. His experience in negotiating arms control is extensive. We welcome him to the Miller Center.

---

[*]*Presented in a Forum at the Miller Center of Public Affairs on 25 February 1992.*

MR. EARLE: I will begin our discussion by talking a little about the budget, which is not, however, my field of expertise. The world is different today than it was a year or two ago, and certainly when I was negotiating the SALT II Treaty in that confrontational superpower relationship. The world is still uncertain, but we know it is different. We have to rethink many things like strategic policy, budget policy, conversion, and so forth.

In its defense budget, the administration is asking for $291 billion, which is not significantly less than the budget was during the height of the Cold War. It is seeking $50 billion in reductions over the next five years. That is about 3 percent a year, which is not, in my view, significant. It is possible to do considerably more than that, given the virtual elimination of the Soviet threat and the total absence of the Warsaw Pact threat.

The enemy that we faced for 45 years isn't there anymore. So how much do we really need to budget for defense? I think we could probably cut an additional $100 billion or a total of $30 billion reduction per year over the next five years. The major reductions will come in manpower, the most expensive item in the defense budget. In Desert Storm, we applied 20 percent of our defense assets. If we could defeat the fourth largest army in the world with only 20 percent of our assets, we don't really need to maintain current force levels. We can probably make further cuts beyond the five-year period for a 50 percent total reduction.

There are problems, of course, as has been reported in newspapers recently. Morale in the military is down because people who enlisted and received commissions with a view to being career soldiers or sailors are now facing unemployment. These things have to be taken into consideration, and that may be one of the reasons why the proposed reductions were so modest. Most of the proposed savings will come from two things: terminating the B-2 bomber program at 20 aircraft and canceling the Seawolf submarine program after one ship. We aren't cutting much elsewhere.

The subject that I would like to address particularly in the budget and in the whole strategic context is the issue of the Strategic Defense Initiative (SDI) and the Anti-Ballistic Missile (ABM) situation. A little history is appropriate, because there are many misunderstandings in this area.

In 1969 when the first Strategic Arms Limitation Talks (SALT) started with the Soviet Union, both sides had begun to or were about to begin MIRVing—putting multiple independently targetable reentry vehicles on top of their missiles. This meant that one missile could carry 10 to 14 warheads, each separately targeted. MIRVs were developed because both sides were building missile defenses, and additional warheads were perceived as necessary to overwhelm these defenses.

During the first negotiations—the SALT I talks—the ABM Treaty was signed and eventually ratified by the Senate in 1972. This treaty limited missile defenses to two sites. One could defend the national command authority and one could defend a missile field. In 1974 an amendment or protocol to that treaty reduced defenses to one site.

The United States built and deployed missile defenses with 100 launchers, the maximum permitted, at Grand Forks Air Force Base in North Dakota. The Soviets, in effect, had their cake and ate it too, because they deployed defenses in Moscow, their national command authority. The missile fields near Moscow were also covered, so they got two-for-one. These weren't good missile defenses. The Soviets still have theirs, called the Galosh system. They have upgraded it to 100 launchers, rather ineffective against the United States' 12,000 deliverable strategic warheads. The United States decided its defenses were ineffective, and eventually removed most of the equipment at Grand Forks. For years, the only effective defense against missiles has been deterrence—each side knew if it attacked the other, it would be destroyed in the exchange.

The missile defense issue returned in 1983 when President Reagan made his famous "Star Wars" speech, in which he advocated the construction, development, and deployment of a system that would make nuclear weapons obsolete. Interestingly, to my knowledge, this is the only presidential decision in the Reagan administration that really began in the Oval Office. There was almost no staffing support for the decision. The Pentagon was as stunned by that speech as was everyone else.

The Soviets were concerned because they thought we knew something they didn't. They eventually learned that we didn't know anything more than they did. By now everyone has accepted that the "Star Wars" dream of President Reagan was just that—a dream. It would be absolutely impossible to achieve a situation in which there was an umbrella over the United States that would prevent any single warhead from entering. It has great appeal, however, and Congress has supported it with funds ranging from $3 billion to $5 billion per year. Prior to March 1983 when Reagan's speech was made, we had been spending almost $1 billion a year on research and development of ballistic missile defense (BMD). BMD was not forgotten, and we stayed current with the state of the art. It was a wise expenditure. In my view, however, not all monies have been spent wisely as we switch from one plan to another for ballistic missile defense.

Support in Congress was waning, and funding was gradually reduced, with the administration consistently getting less than it requested. Then an event that is not relevant, but seemed to be, occurred: the Gulf War and the Scud-Patriot duels we saw on television with the dramatic lights in the sky and explosions. SDI proponents seized upon that as an indication, or indeed hard evidence, that ballistic missile defenses were feasible and necessary.

To comment on the Scud-Patriot duel, first of all, the Patriot was an old technology. Actually, when I joined NATO in 1969, we were developing something called SAM-D, which was a surface-to-air missile for use against aircraft. After it went through a number of iterations, it was converted to Patriot, our first ballistic missile defender. Patriot was developed as a point defense system to protect a specific site: an airfield, a headquarters, or something like that. It was never considered an effective area defense. Scud missile technology dates even further back than Patriot.

It now appears that in spite of the initial enthusiasm at Raytheon, the Patriot wasn't effective. Only an estimated 20 percent of the missiles were effective, which means that 80 percent of the Scuds launched got through. The Scuds were ineffective simply because they were inaccurate and frequently broke up in flight, not because of anything the Patriot did.

This was an example, in my view, of a failure in the Patriot. It was put under an unfair burden, however, because it was turned into a quasi-area defense system to protect Israeli cities. Obviously, it couldn't sustain that burden. The point, though, is not whether it was a success. The point is that it is wrongly perceived as an indication that there can be defenses against in-coming ballistic missiles. It just isn't related to that. While the Patriot may have diverted a number of Scuds, those Scuds had conventional warheads. Facing a real strategic missile threat with nuclear warheads, the diversion to Georgetown of a strategic warhead aimed at the White House won't do much good.

Public perception made the Patriot a highly political issue, and resulted immediately in renewed congressional interest in the development of a Strategic Defense Initiative. Senators John Warner and Sam Nunn proposed a nice compromise bill. It troubles me that it was passed without any hearings or real study of the issues. Basically, the Nunn-Warner bill calls for rebuilding the 100 launchers at Grand Forks within the permissible context of the ABM Treaty. A system with much more sophisticated missiles, guidance systems, and detection systems would be able to protect the central one-third of the United States from a random, limited attack. The perceived threat here is twofold: an accidental launch (the *Red October* scenario gone even more aberrational) or an unintentional launch (somebody pushes the wrong button and a missile comes towards the United States). Frankly, I find both scenarios quite unlikely, but they have been discussed for years.

The Nunn-Warner approach has something in it for everyone. For those who like the ABM Treaty and don't want to see it altered and who believe that ballistic-missile system defenses are impractical, it keeps the ABM Treaty intact. I like that portion of it. For those who want upgrading of the Patriot, I don't think anyone will deny that we need a point defense system against conventional warheads for our forces overseas. Their proposal calls for upgrading the Patriot. For those who are all-out fans of the Strategic Defense Initiative and still believe in the original dream, like Senator Malcolm Wallop, it is the camel's nose under the tent. Once we begin building defenses, we can either break out of the ABM Treaty or negotiate with Russia about enlarging the permissible systems.

The estimated cost of the Grand Forks site with 100 missiles alone ranges from $10 to $26 billion. If we were to add two more sites, one in Maine and one in the state of Washington, in an effort to protect the United States from random launches, it could range up to $60 billion. As Senator Everett Dirksen said, "A billion here and a billion there, and after a while, you've run into real money."

This calls for an analysis of the threat, which is debatable. Heretofore the threat was the Soviet Union with its thousands of deliverable strategic warheads. I think that threat is basically gone. The recent talks that Undersecretary Reginald Bartholomew and Secretary James Baker had with the various republics are encouraging. The warheads are being separated from the missiles. There will still be some threat, but it looks like the control will be as centralized in Russia as it was in the Soviet Union. The threat of an all-out attack is no more real than it was when the Soviet Union was centrally run.

What about the Third World? The Director of Central Intelligence Robert Gates recently said that the chance of any Third World country obtaining a missile that could strike the United States is at least 15 years away. I would hope that in 15 years we could take some steps of a nonmilitary nature that would reduce the threat of Third World ballistic missiles—either restrictions on transfer of technology or missiles, simple negotiations, or demonstration of the wisdom of not having these weapons.

So delivery systems—in a military sense—as far as the United States is concerned don't exist and won't exist. It will still be difficult for us to defend against a nuclear bomb on a ship in New York harbor or an aircraft coming from another country on an apparently innocent mission. U.S. borders with Canada and Mexico are leaky. I doubt that someone who wanted to launch a short-range missile from the back of a truck in Mexico would have much difficulty doing so. That kind of option would not be covered by the proposed Grand Forks defense system.

There are other ways. Congress passed a bill sponsored by Senator Nunn and Les Aspin, the chairman of the House Armed Services Committee, that initially called for $1 billion in aid to the former Soviet Union. They were forced to accept $500 million: $100 million in humanitarian aid and $400 million in aid to fund missile dismantlement. That is a small amount, however, and this is an expensive business. In addition to missiles, there are nuclear warheads, chemical weapons, and biological weapons.

When we talk about dollars, I'm reminded of the money we spent on our defense budget over the years. If someone had come to us two years ago and said, "What will you pay for the breakup of the Soviet Union, the elimination of the Berlin Wall, and the willingness on the part of the Soviet leadership to dismantle almost all, if not all, of their weapons?", we would have paid unimaginable sums. Now we are paying $400 million to help them eliminate their weapons. I think we should spend a lot more on Soviet aid and a lot less on building four more B-2 bombers. Four more bombers will cost $4 billion. Imagine, $1 billion for one airplane! I think there are better ways to spend our money. My view is that $2 billion instead of the $5.4 billion requested this year would be sufficient for ballistic missile defense. That would pay for upgrading the Patriot and the necessary research and development to continue staying with the state of the art.

The real issue is that we haven't analyzed the threat. Why do we need the 10,000 nuclear weapons that we will have after implementing the START Treaty, or even the 5,000 that the President and Secretary Baker say we can go to? Unquestionably, we can't eliminate them all. The genie is out of the bottle. The scientists know how to do it. Even 15 years ago, a Princeton undergraduate used unclassified sources to write an accurate paper detailing how to build a nuclear weapon. Nuclear weapons are going to be an issue for a long time, if not forever. Perhaps, as was suggested earlier, they have deterred attacks and might well continue to do so.

Ideally, I would like to see the segregation of weapons from their delivery systems. We are not going to eliminate them, and it would be upsetting if we got rid of all of ours and then Gadhafi said, "Tee-hee, I've got three!" That number of weapons would be enough for him to blackmail us in a nuclear fashion. I think there is movement in our discussions with the former Soviet republics toward this type of segregation.

The elimination of a nuclear weapon is complicated and expensive, as is the elimination of chemical weapons. Over a year ago, when we were negotiating a bilateral chemical weapons treaty with the Soviets, they indicated that they feared they could not agree to our proposed timetable and criteria for destruction, because even then they could not afford it. It is expensive.

Maybe we can't afford to do it all at once, but we can pursue segregation, something the non-Russian republics are already doing. They are removing the warheads from the delivery systems and taking them to Russia for storage. All the nuclear weapons in the world could be segregated if there were satisfactory inspection procedures. Obviously, it won't happen tomorrow, and it may never happen, but it is a thought.

COMMENT: A recent speaker commented on the elimination of warheads. He said that it would be preferable to separate the warhead from the delivery vehicle but then do nothing more because it would be more hazardous. He also said there is a gradual deterioration in the effectiveness of the weapon, and over a period of time it would become useless. However, if the warhead were taken apart, the plutonium could be a valuable and dangerous thing.

MR. EARLE: It's a good point. I am not a nuclear physicist, so I cannot talk about deterioration. I know that they do deteriorate and that the tritium which enhances its yield vanishes. Loose plutonium could be used by others, so my mind is open on that. I would like to do something to prevent accidental detonation. That can be done without having to remove the fissionable material. Basically, they become unarmed, and that may be the solution. Then they would be kept in secure sites so you wouldn't have to worry about loose plutonium.

QUESTION: How would we negotiate changes in these treaties or new ones? Would we have to negotiate them with all of the republics of the former Soviet Union?

MR. EARLE: That is a good question, and one that has given lawyers in Washington a great deal of opportunity to work in the last few months. I think you can make the argument that the treaties in existence now are binding on the successor state—Russia—and Russia has agreed to that. I would still like to get their signature so that there can't be any question about it.

Two of the other three nuclear republics, Belarus and Ukraine, have been assured by us that we do not consider them nuclear powers simply because they have nuclear weapons on their territory, just as Germany, Italy, and many other of our allies have. They agreed that they will become parties to the Non-Proliferation Treaty (NPT) as nonnuclear-weapon states. Kazakhstan has been a little fuzzy, but we are hopeful that they will do the same. I would also like to get republic signatures on the NPT and other existing treaties, and they said they would do that. For future treaties the negotiations would obviously have to be conducted on an individual basis. I don't think the CIS (Commonwealth of Independent States) is perceived as having the authority to negotiate binding agreements for any of its members.

The signatories have to have agreements among themselves. In the Intermediate-range Nuclear Forces Treaty (INF), because of the on-site inspection provisions, each of the parties had to have a bilateral treaty with each of the inspecting parties. In other words, Holland, where we had nuclear cruise missiles, had to negotiate a treaty with the Soviet Union and another Warsaw Pact country that was going to be an inspector in Holland. It is complicated, but it can be done if the parties want to have an agreement.

QUESTION: Recently, there has been a great deal of interest in expanding nonproliferation, and that is hopeful. I am worried, however, that collaboration with Soviet scientists, while keeping them employed, might increase proliferation substantively. In other words, what information will American and Soviet scientists exchange? Knowledge on how to improve delivery systems? Knowledge on how to make bigger and better weapons of destruction? How do you prevent this exchange of information from contributing to weapons proliferation?

MR. EARLE: First, I would rather have Soviet scientists sharing their knowledge with us than with Libyan scientists. Second, you need money to build these things. If the scientists sit and draw diagrams, I don't think any serious harm has been done. It is only harmful if you fund the actual development, testing, and creation of them, and I would hope that we could control that.

MR. GEORGE PERKOVICH: The scientists are discussing fiberoptics, magnetic fusion, waste management and cleanup, and medical uses of nuclear technology, but the security part has been segregated out for many of the reasons that you mentioned. Interesting proposals include doing weapon safety work together, but that hasn't received government approval yet.

There is an interesting effect when you store these warheads called the popcorn effect. When a bunch of warheads are stored in an "igloo," if one of them has a sudden neutron flux, it is like popcorn in a popper, theoretically. American weapons experts don't know how to prevent or deal with that. They speculate that the Russians have no idea either. That is one area they want to address collaboratively, but the government hasn't decided whether they can share that kind of information. We are entering a weird new world where people are saying, "There is something I have really been concerned about over all these years, and I would love to work on it with the Russians."

QUESTION: Are we currently storing the warheads in what might be a popcorn popper?

MR. PERKOVICH: A former assistant secretary of defense said it has been a theoretical problem that involves storing large numbers of warheads together. That hasn't happened in the United States yet. The Russians are stuffing tactical weapons into storage facilities. They lack additional storage capacity and want to use the $400 million in aid to build it. Previously, they stored the weapons in the republics where they were deployed. Now they are bringing them back to Russia and do not know where to store them.

MR. EARLE: Russia has always been, to the best of our knowledge, very careful about command, control, and storage of its nuclear weapons. It is suggested now, however, that they are having to cram them into the closet. The closet is almost full, so they may have some problems.

COMMENT: In the context of public debates on cutting defense, the lead times in developing superior conventional armaments are so long that it becomes very difficult to actually reduce military spending to some arbitrary levels. Long lead times mean you have to be ready before your opponent is ready.

MR. EARLE: I once remarked to a former colleague of mine in the Pentagon that the night vision, the accuracy of the weapons, and so forth of today's technology had a staggering effect in the Gulf War. He said, "Today's technology? That was Harold Brown's technology. Wait till you see what we are developing now!" Harold Brown was the defense secretary 12 years ago. In other words, all those things we used in the Gulf War were already on the board. The United States must do two things: maintain its research and development (R&D) base for devising new prototypes and upgrade what it already has. For example, do we need a new fighter, or can we upgrade the black boxes on the F-15, the finest fighter in the world today? Many joke that the B-52s are older than the people who fly them, but they have been upgraded so often that they are almost entirely different airplanes. Only the airframe is the same. Hopefully the current world climate of openness will create opportunities for political restraints on the technology race.

QUESTION: You argued that the $400 million that is currently available to aid Russia in dismantling their weapons is insufficient. What would be an appropriate amount and what are the political realities of getting that money and applying it?

MR. EARLE: John Parachini, who accompanied me, might have an idea of the necessary amount of funding.

MR. PARACHINI: Some people have proposed 1 percent of the defense budget or $3 billion per year, but no one really knows what the real need is. The Russians haven't even determined an effective way to deal with the chemical weapons portion, about which the debate in the United States has been fairly brisk. The former Soviet republics don't have anywhere near the level of technology that we do. At the high end, people have chosen the $3 billion mark, which is 1 percent for peace and dismantlement, but a full cost assessment of that doesn't really exist. The executive branch is not sure how to use the $400 million, and Congress is concerned about spending that $400 million on studies as opposed to weapons dismantlement. It is a challenge that requires much greater attention by the Congress and the executive branch.

QUESTION: Given that we have hungry people and countries that are accustomed to revolution, are we spending enough time and energy on how to feed the people to prevent them from revolting before we have put disarmament into effect?

MR. EARLE: In my view, we are not spending enough. This is a window of opportunity that has never existed before, and with the possibility of unrest and even civil war in Russia, it may not last. Some worry about war between Russia and Ukraine, but there are enough problems within Russia. I don't think we are doing nearly enough for our own self interest, and we are behind the Germans. In Eastern Europe the Germans are becoming dominant in terms of influence in the new economy. We are way behind. In the eastern part of what used to be the Soviet Union, the Japanese are moving in and we are seen as dragging our feet.

In an election year when you have unemployed and homeless people in the United States, it is tough to spend money on Russians or Kazakhs or Uzbeks, but the opportunity isn't going to last forever. We will just have to bite the bullet and do much more than we are doing. I am concerned about the possibility of losing this opportunity.

QUESTION: As a policy matter, why should our objective not be the elimination of national nuclear forces and the internationalization of a small deterrent force?

MR. EARLE: "Should" makes the question much harder to answer than "can" or "would." It is difficult for me to envisage this country or any other country at this stage of our development putting nuclear weapons in the hands of an international organization without our having control over them. Politically, it would be hard for the country to swallow, and therefore for any president to do.

I have my own reservations, but maybe that is because I am somewhat of a chauvinist. Can you really trust an international body? Who is going to oversee them? Look at what the United Nations went through until recently with the Third World and the group of 77 that, although not dominant, made life difficult for American diplomats. It is an ideal solution, but it is like the benevolent despot. Where do you find him? I'm leery of it. Of course I would be happy if all the nuclear weapons in the world, except those of the United States, were given to the United Nations, but I would hesitate to give up American weapons.

QUESTION: We have read a great deal of press reporting on the inadequacies of the International Atomic Energy Agency's (IAEA) efforts to safeguard nuclear materials and facilities that might be used to produce nuclear materials. Do you have any opinions as to whether this activity, which I see as one of the most important functions of any international organization in the coming years, should remain with IAEA or reside with another, more powerful agency? Realistically, do you think there is a chance for an effective safeguard regime?

MR. EARLE: As an agency, IAEA is fine, but it lacks two things: sufficient funding and sufficient authority. According to Mr. Parachini, the current budget of the IAEA, the inspection agency under the Non-Proliferation Treaty, approximately equals that of the Dallas police force. The United States should lead the effort to increase IAEA funding and the number of inspectors. We need to expand the inspection regime beyond its current Non-Proliferation Treaty level where only declared sites are inspected. The IAEA can't inspect undeclared sites, and those are the ones we worry about. We have to put more teeth into the NPT and the IAEA and then increase funding.

COMMENT: According to a Russian acquaintance, the average physician in Russia earns 300 rubles a month, a school teacher about 600, and a laborer 900. With the open society, that leads me to wonder if Russian scientists will sell themselves abroad, having been so underpriced in the Russian market.

MR. EARLE: That is a strong threat, I think. I recently read that they had sold part of the Black Sea fleet to India. I don't know how that happened. The Russians did it, not the Ukrainians. We have to find something for these people to do because they have family obligations, and with the constant devaluation of the ruble, if Gadhafi offered them a villa on the Mediterranean and a couple of hundred dollars a month, it would be rather appealing.

MR. PERKOVICH: It is in the Russians' interest to raise such warnings, as they did a couple of months ago. They got the $400 million, and now the lab directors are saying their people are responsible, so they won't sell out to get rich abroad. It is an interesting dynamic. We are receiving mixed signals from them.

QUESTION: Will we really be able to expand the Non-Proliferation Treaty if national governments continue to retain their nuclear weapons, and will proliferation increase if we keep our weapons?

MR. EARLE: Actually, there have been many encouraging events in the proliferation regime in recent years. Argentina and Brazil have quit their competition, and South Africa has declared that it will sign and abide by the NPT. On the other hand, Pakistan has clearly gone nuclear while we have been complaining about them and they have been lying to us. North Korea is a serious threat. Israel obviously already has nuclear weapons. Iraq was much closer than we thought.

QUESTION: Could you really expect restraint from the Arabs, who will be a bit stronger than they are now?

MR. EARLE: Again, we get into the realm of politics. At the conference on the Limited Test Ban Treaty last January in New York—which got no publicity because it happened to convene the day the war started—the Israelis said they wanted a nuclear-free zone in the Middle East, preconditioned on recognition and an overall peace treaty. As long as some of us, and particularly the Israelis, hang on to the bomb, the neighbors are going to seek parity. It is the same situation in the subcontinent with the Pakistanis and the Indians. The Pakistanis talk about a nuclear-free zone and the Indians talk about a nuclear-free world. Nonproliferation is a very serious concern at this time. The IAEA is important, but I think we have to force the issue. The Non-Proliferation Treaty comes up for major review in 1995. We are facing a real problem. We want, I assume, to extend it indefinitely, but one of the preconditions of many nations attending that conference is the cessation, or at least a moratorium, on testing. This administration so far has refused to consider that. It is a significant problem.

QUESTION: The IAEA, to my understanding, does have statutory authority to inspect undeclared facilities in the countries of NPT signatories. I think this is a position that Hans Blix has been trying to push. My question is related to targeting. According to what I have read recently, the Defense Department is doing some selective retargeting away from the former Soviet Union to other undeclared countries. I would be interested in your comment on that.

MR. EARLE: I wrote an op-ed article on that very issue. Actually, it's not the Defense Department. That department empowered a panel of people previously in government but who were then out of government. They proposed some absurd ideas: for instance, a nuclear expeditionary force roaming the world and targeting every conceivable adversary. If nuclear weapons weren't used against Saddam Hussein, then what adversary would we *ever* use them against? I don't think that this proposal has carried much weight in the Department of Defense. The issue of targeting is one that we have to address. Before we decide to go from 10,000 to 5,000, or even from 5,000 to 1,000, we should determine what our needs are. What do we want to target?

I was at the Strategic Air Command headquarters in Omaha where the Single Integrated Operational Plan (SIOP) was developed. When you have 12,000 deliverable warheads, it is hard to find targets. I looked at the American targets. After you put two warheads on each silo and you have two on one of the hardened command and control facilities as well as the dockyards, shipyards, major military staging areas, airfields, and anti-aircraft, there are still several thousand warheads left. You really have to scratch your head to find targets.

We need a completely new analysis of our targeting related to our policy. Once we determine our policy, we determine our targets, and then we can say that we need 482 warheads, or 4,082 warheads. It is similar to the 600-ship Navy. I always wondered why it wasn't 602 ships or 598 ships. It was just an arbitrary goal.

NARRATOR: We want to thank all of you, and particularly Ambassador Earle, for his characteristically clear, courageous, and forceful presentation.

CHAPTER THREE

Presidents and Arms Control: Process and Incidents*

RAYMOND GARTHOFF

NARRATOR: Dr. Raymond Garthoff is one of the world's foremost authorities on arms control; he is also an expert on the Soviet Union. He is senior fellow at the Brookings Institution in its Foreign Policy Studies Program and was an ambassador in the Carter administration.

He had major responsibility for arms control in the Kennedy, Johnson, and Nixon administrations. He was an official in the Eisenhower administration responsible for drafting estimates on Soviet foreign policy and strategy. In 1958, he drafted the first comprehensive National Intelligence Estimate.

Dr. Garthoff is a universally respected senior scholar. His book *Detente and Confrontation* is a classic to which those of us working in the field of foreign policy continually refer. We welcome him to the Miller Center.

MR. GARTHOFF: I am going to give some comments about the arms control process and the experiences of the various administrations with which I was involved. I can't cover the whole

---

Presented in a Forum at the Miller Center of Public Affairs on 30 October 1991.

history of arms negotiations, but I am going to focus on a number of specific incidents and aspects of the process on which I think I can shed some light and which may provide a basis for discussion.

I will begin with the Eisenhower administration. I was not involved or aware of the action in the early postwar negotiations on the Baruch plan, the failed effort to control nuclear weapons at the outset of the nuclear age. In the Eisenhower administration, both the President and Secretary of State John Foster Dulles had an interest in disarmament and arms reduction. But there was also a strong skepticism—which I think was justified—regarding the Soviet Union's degree of interest in verified arms reductions and disarmament. For that reason, disarmament tended to be regarded more as part of the political warfare and propaganda of the Cold War.

One exception, although it did not lead to agreement, was the possibility of getting a nuclear test ban in the mid-1950s. In fact, the record shows that President Eisenhower and others in the administration were thinking about an initiative toward a comprehensive test ban at the time of the 1956 electoral campaign. For better or for worse, Adlai Stevenson made his own proposals, which were then seen by the administration as a challenge that needed rebutting rather than as an idea that could be supported and developed. That policy argument unfortunately headed off what might otherwise have been an opportunity for even more complete limitations on nuclear testing than were ultimately achieved several years later.

There were sharply divided views within the administration over disarmament. Declassified records published in the last few years in the official *Foreign Relations of the United States* series include a number of NSC meetings and associated memoranda which show that the JCS (Joint Chiefs of Staff) expressed very strong doubt about the desirability of even entering into negotiations. As I have already indicated, neither Secretary Dulles or President Eisenhower took that position, but because of the JCS's deep skepticism, disarmament was really little more than a political exercise.

NARRATOR: Could you speak briefly about your role in preparing the first National Intelligence Estimate?

MR. GARTHOFF: I served in the Office of National Estimates of the Central Intelligence Agency in the second Eisenhower administration, where I was responsible for drafting estimates on Soviet foreign policy and strategy. That included the first Special National Intelligence Estimate on the Soviet attitude toward disarmament, in 1958. We had written estimates of Soviet positions on particular issues in this field earlier, but that was the first overall examination looking into the motivations pro and con in Moscow, the different factors that were influencing Soviet judgment, and the Soviet position in this field. That led, as had these NSC meetings in the mid-1950s, to some dispute and argument. But there was a recognition in that estimate that the Soviet Union had security interests as they saw them, and had reasons of their own both for favoring movement in disarmament and for remaining cautious about the way they did it—in that respect, not entirely unlike our own mix of interests.

We also had a Soviet-American conference on surprise attack in 1958, but it did not lead to anything because the Soviet approach was more political and ours was more technical. The two didn't jibe.

On two occasions, unfortunately, we took positions in the disarmament negotiations, once in 1955 and again in 1959, which the Soviets more or less accepted but which we then repudiated. Repudiating one's own negotiating positions is not a good idea, but it was a question in the first instance of our not following through to find out whether something might have worked out. The Soviets were showing a readiness to accept some degree of on-site inspection, but we don't know for sure even to this day if they were serious. Instead of pursuing that, we drew attention to a new initiative on "Open Skies" that we had made largely for propaganda purposes.

In the other incidents, in 1959 and 1960, the disarmament negotiator, Mr. Harold Stassen, exceeded his instructions, at least in the judgment of those in Washington. The administration then pulled back even further and in effect discontinued serious negotiations.

The early months of the Kennedy administration marked the first overall review by an administration of the whole subject of arms control. A series of panels was convened on different aspects of the problem: one on conventional arms, one on surprise attack, one on what we would now call confidence-building measures, and one on strategic nuclear arms. These were made up of government and outside experts. John J. McCloy was in charge of the overall exercise and that brought some of the academic experts on arms control like Tom Schelling and others from Harvard and RAND, etc., into contact with people in the government. The major upshot of it was the decision to create the Arms Control and Disarmament Agency (ACDA), which was placed under the leadership of William Foster. I had been seconded over from CIA to participate as a member of the panel under General John Hull that worked on conventional arms reductions. We drew up a list of recommendations, as did the other panels. The recommendations then went to the government agencies involved. I went back with a different "hat" and wrote the CIA comments on the paper of which I myself had been a partial author!

I then made a career turn and moved to the Department of State in the fall of 1961 to a new political-military staff. Initially there were about a half dozen of us, whereas today there are approximately 80 to 100 people in the Bureau of Politico-Military Affairs, which is the descendent of our little group. So I was then involved in yet a third capacity on the same project, working on the implementation of some of those proposals.

We had by that time decided that rather than letting the Soviet Union champion "general and complete disarmament," we would also enter with our own broad general proposals. I think that was a wise thing to do. Although it didn't lead to any agreement, at least it stood off the propaganda challenge.

There also was an emerging interest on both sides in what we first called "partial measures"—that is, separate arms control agreements on more limited subjects. These did not lead to any early agreements, but they did point a future direction for arms control and arms reduction arrangements.

One of those proposals, concerning the placement of nuclear weapons in orbit, was rather interesting and unusual in the way that the bureaucracy handled it and in particular in the way President Kennedy did. Both sides had presented rather differing proposals as part of the general disarmament provisions that no one really thought were going to come about. But a separate measure that might well have been agreed upon was quite a different matter. There was a sharper focus on what that would entail and what we should and should not want for reasons of security.

This was the offshoot of a range of studies that were taken on a very secret basis on space policy in general, relating especially to what were at that time highly classified space reconnaissance activities. Our main interest there was to prevent anything that might interfere with that major element of our ability to collect information. We were concerned, for example, about proposals raised within the American government and made by other governments in Geneva disarmament talks and the United Nations for advanced notification and registration of all space launchings and descriptions of the payloads thereof.

As an offshoot of a study that dealt with a number of these questions, there was also a provision raising the possibility of prohibiting orbital deployment of weapons of mass destruction. This was initially presented to the President in terms of objections on the part of all of the agencies. There was no dissent from the consensus opposing a declaratory ban and in favor of a ban on nuclear weapons in space only if it could be adequately monitored. No one was confident that we would be able to work out the provisions, much less get agreement on them for a verification system. Up to that point, this was not atypical.

I was the executive secretary of a special interagency group on space reconnaissance policy, and in the summer of 1962 we sent the recommendations opposing such a ban to the White House. (The subject had already come up once in a Canadian initiative that we had been unable to head off in talks in Geneva.) About a week later I received a call from Carl Kaysen, who was McGeorge Bundy's deputy at NSC in the White House. He said that the President had reviewed the recommendation but was not sure that the group had given adequate consideration to the possible desirability of a ban on nuclear weapons in space even without a verification apparatus. Before signing off on this the President wanted to be sure that we had considered carefully what we had, in effect, deprecated as a mere declaratory ban.

I told Kaysen I did not think in good conscience that we had really considered the pros and cons of the alternative, which we hadn't. The result was that a week or so later a message came back from the President to the secretary of state and others stating that our recommendation was not taken and requesting that the agencies look at the alternative of a ban on placing nuclear weapons in space.

That was very unusual, especially because the initial recommendation had been unanimous. Normally, unanimous recommendations tend to be accepted by a president. It is only when there is a dissent that questions tend to get a sharper, closer look. We looked at the alternative and a few weeks later decided that it *would* be in our interest to have a ban on weapons in space, and that we *would* be able to monitor this adequately with our national means of verification. We switched from a unanimous judgment against the ban to a unanimous view the other way.

You might assume that this was simply a question of the bureaucracy caving into a different viewpoint from the President, but I urge you not to. Instead, it was that we hadn't given sufficient thought to the issue, and the President's request that we do so made the system gear up in a responsive way. We did in fact make approaches to the Soviet Union along this line, but they were not accepted initially. It became clear that they were looking at possible limitations on weapons in space in the framework in which we and they had previously talked. Our approach in the past had been to link intercontinental ballistic missiles that transited space with weapons that were actually stationed in space. The Soviets had held a temporary advantage in ICBMs, but by then it had evaporated. The Soviet response to our position had always been to say that our forward-based missiles and bombers had to be included if their intercontinental missiles were to be counted.

That problem persisted for almost a year, but eventually we got the Soviets to understand that we were not talking about weapons that transited space, but only about weapons placed in

46

orbit. An agreement was then reached in October 1963 and put into effect in a resolution of the United Nations General Assembly, presented and jointly endorsed by the United States and the Soviet Union with supporting statements on national policy.

The Soviets had been ready to conclude a treaty in 1963. President Kennedy felt, however, that after a bruising battle getting Senate approval for the Limited Test Ban Treaty, it was not time to bring up another arms control treaty for review. Senate opposition to the treaty had centered on verification, but this agreement on weapons in space lacked such provisions. It was the President's decision, and also the preference of most of the agencies, that the agreement not be formalized as a treaty. Four years later there was no problem, and the Senate approved, by an 88-to-0 vote, the ratification of a space treaty which included this ban on weapons of mass destruction. The ban had been in effect from 1963 to 1967, but without the force of a treaty commitment.

The Limited Test Ban Treaty in the Kennedy administration was the one major arms control agreement apart from the weapons in space treaty, and was certainly a desirable measure. From the standpoint of many it was, however, a poor second best to a comprehensive test ban, which is again on the agenda for debate today.

Negotiation on a comprehensive test ban in late 1962 and early 1963 came very close to agreement, but there was a real misunderstanding. Khrushchev believed that the American representatives had indicated that we were only concerned about the principle and that two or three inspections a year would suffice. That had been neither the administration's position nor what it had intended to convey to the Soviets, although two prior negotiations had left that impression.

Our position at that time called for ten inspections per year. We brought that down to eight and were prepared to bring it to six or seven. Key figures in Moscow opposed the idea of any inspections, however, and Khrushchev believed that once he had agreed to two or three, that was that. He did not see that number as being open to a bargaining process in which the two sides would eventually arrive at a logical compromise figure of, say, five inspections per year. Consequently, no agreement was reached.

In the Eisenhower administration these matters had been considered through the planning board of the National Security Council and then in the NSC itself. In the Kennedy administration there was a Committee of Principals, chaired by the secretary of state, and including the secretary of defense, the head of the Arms Control Disarmament Agency, the chairman of the Joint Chiefs of Staff, and the director of Central Intelligence. That group had a working body, a committee of deputies, which looked at issues in detail. Only rarely did arms control questions come to the infrequent meetings of the NSC itself.

The Johnson administration generally carried over that practice. Since the beginning of 1962 we had maintained a standing disarmament group in Geneva, initially the Eighteen Nation Disarmament Committee, and later the Conference of the Committee on Disarmament. This took most of the weight of international consideration of these issues from the U.N. General Assembly, although this body continues to discuss arms matters as well.

Beginning in 1964 efforts were made to discuss separately strategic nuclear delivery vehicles, but the proposals that we advanced were, frankly, skewed in our favor and didn't elicit a Soviet response other than defensive ones that were loaded in their favor. We didn't have any real common ground to work on at that time. Late in the Johnson administration this changed because of deliberations over the deployment of an antiballistic missile (ABM) system by the United States. There had been no great enthusiasm in the administration for deploying such a system except among the people involved in research and development. The fact that the Soviet Union was beginning to deploy an ABM system (albeit not a terribly effective one) around Moscow in the mid-to-late 1960s drew more attention to the question.

In 1967 President Johnson decided to go forward with a decision to deploy antiballistic missiles. He perceived, probably incorrectly, a rising interest in ABM deployment in the Senate. Because this was tied so strongly to the fact that the Soviet Union was embarking on an ABM program, the President agreed when Secretary McNamara urged that we make an effort to negotiate a limitation or ban on ABM systems with the Soviet Union before proceeding with ABM development. In December 1966 we approached the Soviet Union on this question. The Soviets responded immediately, saying there should also be a limit on offensive strategic arms. Somewhat to their surprise, we promptly agreed and said that we were prepared to negotiate on the basis of both. This was the beginning of the Strategic Arms Limitations Talks (SALT).

It was a slow beginning; the Soviets repeatedly failed to agree to a specific time or place for starting such negotiations. By the fall of 1967, President Johnson therefore decided to go ahead with the announcement of ABM deployment. He left it to Secretary McNamara, who was strongly opposed, to formulate the presentation. McNamara, however, in his September 1967 speech tied the ABM proposal to a possible ICBM threat from China or accidental launches. We were thus moving toward limited ABM coverage of the country, rather than a heavy deployment intended to blunt the growing Soviet intercontinental ballistic missile threat.

SALT negotiations were finally set to begin in the fall of 1968. Agreement had already been reached for a summit meeting in Leningrad, coincident with the beginning of strategic arms limitation talks in early October 1968. That announcement was going to be made on 21 August. The top secret cables in advance with the information about this had gone out to key embassies so they would be prepared to discuss this announcement with our allies. On the day before that announcement, however, Soviet tanks rolled into Czechoslovakia. Of course, we had to abort and recall that planned announcement, and no negotiations were held, nor any summit meeting, despite efforts by President Johnson to do so after the election. The other development that occurred the same month was the first testing of a MIRVed (multiple independently targeted re-entry vehicle) missile.

The Nixon administration wanted, not unreasonably, to examine the whole picture before launching any negotiations. They wanted to get their own defense program straightened out, including a decision on what kind of ABM to deploy. The result was that the SALT talks didn't begin until November 1969. By that time, however, the United States had completed a very successful test program with MIRV and was almost ready to begin deploying

MIRVed missiles. That effectively prejudiced the possibility of limiting offensive strategic arms in a meaningful way during the SALT negotiations.

Both President Nixon and National Security Adviser Henry Kissinger quickly came to play a key role in such matters, but neither had much interest in arms control as such. It was not that they opposed arms control negotiations, but both tended to look upon them primarily as elements in a broader political game, which, of course, they were. But the negotiations also had an intrinsic importance that was sometimes not given due regard.

NARRATOR: In the Nixon oral history that we have done, much emphasis has been placed on the fact that Nixon tried to get his foreign policy team in place before he chose people for any other position. Leonard Garment, for instance, has been here and talked about the part that he played in advising Nixon and helping to look for people. Were the arms control people similarly picked early and regarded with high priority?

MR. GARTHOFF: No. It wasn't that there was any great delay in selecting the top arms control people—primarily Ambassador Gerard Smith, who headed the ACDA and managed the SALT negotiations. Yet there definitely was a decision to hold back from making any decisions about arms control policy initiatives or holding negotiations until after defense policy had been worked out.

I think it would have been a mistake to make decisions on arms control policy before making decisions on defense policy. No one was advocating that. On the other hand, to some extent it was a mistake to wait until after defense policy had been set and then look at the arms control picture, because arms control is one facet of security policy along with defense policy and programs. Without saying it should be given any priority, it ought to be a consideration in conjunction with decisions on defense programs and policies.

In the case of SALT there was quite an anomaly because the Nixon administration had decided to proceed with a nationwide "thin" ABM deployment program. Yet when it came to drawing up the first SALT proposals regarding ABMs at the beginning of 1970, the two options given attention were for either a total ban on ABMs or for defending national capitals only (the Soviets would keep their ABMs deployed around Moscow, and we would deploy a system around Washington). That would have a certain logic in terms of protecting the national command authorities against any accidental launch, for example, without getting into the complexities involved in doing that for the whole country.

There was a disjunction between the objectives of the Nixon ABM program spelled out in the spring of 1969 and the early proposals Nixon authorized for the American SALT negotiators. The program Nixon submitted to Congress called for four ABM sites, and after a bruising fight on the Hill, it was passed by one or two votes in both 1969 and 1970. We had nothing on the table in the SALT talks, however, that resembled the administration's legislative programs at the time. The Soviets quickly agreed as soon as we had mentioned the possibility of restricting ABMs to one site, in the spring of 1970. They didn't want to give up the Moscow system by agreeing on zero ABMs, which was the other proposal we later raised. Nor did they want to see any broader deployment by the United States, since they had no interest in such a system for themselves. Thus, they were quite content with the defense of capitals, which we had offered, but it didn't fit our program.

We went through an odd charade over the proposals we were discussing in 1970 and 1971, next calling for four deployment sites for ourselves while the Soviets would be limited to one. That came around to four and four, then three and three. It was quite clear a year before the agreement was finally reached that it was going to end up, if it ended up anywhere, with either one or two sites on each side. That is what did happen. But for an extended period we were arguing for very artificial positions, only so that it could be said on the Hill that the four sites for which funding was requested were consistent with the arms control proposal that we had on the table.

The effort to control MIRVs was essentially prejudiced by our successful development program. Nonetheless, in the spring of 1970 the United States and the Soviet Union each did make proposals for limiting MIRVs, neither of which were satisfactory to the other party. We proposed bans on either testing or deployment of MIRVs. The ban on deployment was the bottom line at which we aimed. The ban on testing was essential from our standpoint for monitoring and verifying that the Soviets were not going to be able to get a deployable MIRV.

There was a hole in our position that the Soviets had covered in theirs. They wanted a ban on production and deployment of MIRVs. They opposed restrictions on testing, because they wanted to test their own MIRVs to catch up with us. We opposed a ban on production mainly for verification reasons, not because we secretly wanted to produce MIRVs. From the Soviet standpoint, it was quite unsatisfactory to let us continue to produce large numbers of MIRVs and simply hold back from actually putting them on missiles in silos, an option they would not have because they had not yet developed a system that could be produced. The SALT delegation sought to fill in the gap in our position by adding a ban on production but was unable to get approval for this from Washington.

We also were asking for on-site inspection, something that had not been part of the original studies, and in fact we hadn't even made the studies to know how an on-site inspection system might work. That also killed the idea from the Soviet standpoint because they believed that we were not serious about it. In fact, we weren't serious. From then on neither side discussed MIRVs for the rest of the SALT talks.

When the newly sworn President Ford met with Soviet Secretary Brezhnev in Vladivostok in the fall of 1974 they did reach agreement on a basis for a SALT II accord, but they didn't tie down all of the points. A couple of those issues soon presented obstacles. One dispute had to do with cruise missiles, which we were then beginning to develop, and the other was whether the Soviet Backfire bomber should be counted as a heavy bomber. That dragged on over the next year, and as the gap was beginning to be closed by early 1976, President Ford decided, in effect, to drop negotiations, although they continued in a desultory way. Real efforts to reach an agreement were hampered because of the controversies over detente and arms control in the electoral campaign—first in the primaries by Governor Reagan and then in the general election campaign with Jimmy Carter. During the campaign Mr. Carter sounded several different notes, sometimes strongly in favor of arms control and detente and sometimes negative. This fluctuation was due partly to the wide array of advice he was receiving and partly because it was an electoral campaign.

The Carter administration made a proposal in March 1977 for a more ambitious SALT II agreement than the nearly completed one that had been languishing at the end of the Ford administration. This proposal ran counter to assurances that the Soviet leaders thought they had been given by representatives of the President-elect that we were going to pick up where the prior negotiations had been. Instead, they were suddenly presented with a much broader proposed agreement, not only in negotiations in Moscow but also publicly. From their standpoint this not only involved deeper reductions and other considerations that they might want to study, but it also upset the Vladivostok understanding with President Ford. As a result, it set back negotiations in SALT for a number of months. By the time that the SALT II agreement was finally wrapped up in the summer of 1979, it faced some other obstacles and eventually was shelved after the Soviet invasion of Afghanistan. After the spring of 1977, when I completed three years as a senior Foreign Service inspector, I did not return to the arms control field, but began serving as ambassador to Bulgaria.

NARRATOR: Do you know whether others who remained had any hand in Carter's drastic cut plan, or was that held very tightly by a few people?

MR. GARTHOFF: At that time, in February and March 1977, I was still in Washington and was peripherally involved. Some people believed that the Soviets might respond positively, and then it would be a much greater accomplishment if agreement could be reached on that basis. If not, we could fall back to something more modest. There were a couple of problems with that. One was that the Soviet leaders felt they had been misled as to what to expect and weren't in the mood for a rapid shift. The second was that the fallback position that we went to was essentially the one we had taken in the beginning of 1975, rather than the position as it had been reached when the negotiations essentially lapsed in early 1976, so that we offered something less.

This was not adequately appreciated at the time, but I think the main factor actually was that both President Carter and Zbig Brzezinski wanted to take the initiative by going far beyond what the Ford administration had been working on. They did not recognize the hazards in taking that approach.

QUESTION: To what extent were your estimates influenced by having Colonel Penkovskiy as a spy?

MR. GARTHOFF: The material that Colonel Penkovskiy provided from April 1961 until October 1962 was very valuable in a number of respects. Among other things, it helped give us precisely the sort of information on Soviet missile systems that our other sources such as overhead photography could not provide. Putting the two together—having the manuals and other information from human intelligence that you can't see with any camera—was very helpful.

As far as our military estimates were concerned, it helped in a number of other respects. Regarding foreign policy, Colonel Penkovskiy was not as fully informed. One example, the key area in which he had something to say, was the Berlin crisis in the summer of 1961. He did not provide information on the missiles in Cuba, so we were unable to anticipate the Cuban missile crisis. He was arrested on the day that the Cuban missile crisis began because he had been under suspicion for some time. As soon as President Kennedy's speech announced the quarantine and established that there was a crisis over the Soviet missiles in Cuba, the Soviets moved on Penkovskiy immediately.

The colonel provided information on other aspects of Soviet foreign policy and arms control policy as well. Part of it was corridor gossip that he would pick up. Some of it he may have believed; some of it other people may have believed, but nonetheless it was not always correct. It was a mixed bag. But overall, the documentary material and technical information he provided on Soviet military thinking and weaponry was extremely valuable.

QUESTION: Could you share some of your thoughts with us on the rapid changes that have taken place in the last few months?

54

MR. GARTHOFF: The old problems have mostly been solved or swept from the board, and now we have new ones. We are no longer so concerned about whether Gorbachev will agree to this or that kind of political arrangement or arms control agreement as we are in knowing whether he will be in power and who is going to be in a position to deliver on commitments. In addition, it is almost certain that the unilateral reductions in Soviet armed forces, not necessarily in the strategic missile forces, are going to be very substantial, simply because the combination of economic straits and political difficulties are forcing them to reduce considerably.

It is important to note that Gorbachev was prepared to agree to dismantle the Soviet preponderance in conventional arms facing Europe several years ago when he was not even under that kind of pressure. The deal was going to be equality between the two alliances, which is the way the Conventional Forces in Europe (CFE) Agreement was drawn up. By the time it was actually signed, there was in effect no Warsaw Pact, and now there is none at all. The armies of the Eastern European countries are certainly not allies of the Soviet Union, and the Soviet Union under the terms of the treaty has inferior levels of conventional arms in the whole of the European U.S.S.R. vis-à-vis NATO.

It is a different story now. The United States, NATO, as well as the Soviet Union and the other countries in Europe are all reducing arms. It is still desirable that the CFE Treaty be ratified and go into effect, if for no other reason than having verification monitoring personnel there and giving reassurances on all sides that there won't be any massive buildup unless a treaty commitment is breached.

We are now faced with a situation in which it is unclear whether there will be a new union to maintain central control over the elements of military power, what kinds of armed forces the individual republics of the Soviet Union will have, and in particular, how the existing military assets of the Soviet Union—especially nuclear—will be controlled and distributed.

The reductions called for under the CFE and START Agreement are helpful in this respect. The Soviets could and should make as part of their reductions under the START Agreement those ICBMs that are in northern Kazakhstan, the

Ukraine, and Byelorussia. Most of their ICBMs are in Russia, where there is at least a clearer control line. That is still less of a problem than there would be in having several nuclear powers, especially if they have serious political friction or even conflicts among themselves.

Apart from strategic weapons, there are a large number of tactical nuclear weapons, including air defense missile warheads for the air force distributed among a number of the republics, but in especially large numbers in Ukraine and Byelorussia. I think that is going to work out, but it will remain a source of some concern until it is settled.

QUESTION: Has there ever been a study as to the minimum number of nuclear weapons it would take to deter the Soviets? I would be interested in your comments on the possibility of significant additional unilateral reductions by the United States without any loss of security.

MR. GARTHOFF: President Carter asked the Joint Chiefs of Staff in one of his first meetings with them in 1977 to study the possibility of reducing the deterrent forces on both sides to 200 warheads. That study was never really completed, and there were no moves in any other administration to consider reductions on that scale. In the last couple of years there have been official and unofficial studies in both the United States and in Moscow about this question of the minimum reliable deterrent needed. The range of views is between 600 and 3,000 warheads on each side.

The START Agreement calls for a level of 6,000, but that only includes certain defined systems. Because of counting rules, a bomber capable of carrying various combinations of air-launched cruise missiles and gravity bombs is counted as having only one warhead. Cruise missiles are counted in a somewhat different way, but also at nominal rather than full loads. In addition to that kind of distortion, the United States insisted on the exclusion of sea-launched cruise missiles from the 6,000 limit, even though we are not unilaterally converting SLCMs to a conventional role. Thus, we will have between 6,000 and 9,000 warheads in the United States, and the Soviets will have between 5,000 and 8,000 if they go up to the maximum under the START Agreement with its nominal limit of 6,000 warheads. Some people had been thinking about cutting that again by half, however, which would make the limit about 3,000 nominal and maybe 5,000 actual. Studies of what are required seem to depend on how rigorous the assumptions are with respect to the number of nuclear weapons that any country could absorb in a second strike and still function at all as a society. That has rarely been worked through. Such studies have been mostly a matter of determining the numbers of weapons needed to kill residual and strategic forces as well as command-control centers.

Reductions depend on the composition of forces as well, and are much facilitated if multiple warhead systems are reduced or eliminated. If you've got it down to single warhead missiles, then it isn't even important whether they are mobile or silo-fixed. There is no point in using one of your own missiles to kill one of the enemy's missiles if you have equal forces to begin with: You still have equal forces.

Thus, the 3,000 warhead requirement is a rather conservative estimate, that is, larger than needed. There are studies that have been made by the National Academy of Sciences and by others which suggest a minimum deterrent force of between 600 and 2,000 warheads. That is the general range that people are thinking about now. Some people have been proposing moving to 1,000 on each side. I don't think there would be any difficulty getting Soviet agreement to these low figures, but that is not the only consideration.

QUESTION: The Kennedy-McNamara dialogue in which McNamara said 500-1,000 missiles was sufficient but Congress demanded more and McNamara was sent back up to the Hill to testify—is that accurately reported by historians? Wasn't it 1,000 weapons, and then for political reasons McNamara had to agree that more were needed?

MR. GARTHOFF: There were two things. One was a figure of 200-megaton equivalent on targets, and another was the ability to destroy about 25 percent of industry and 30 percent of population, and you could do that with a couple of hundred weapons on target, requiring a larger force.

It is a different matter if you are looking at counterforce requirements, but if you are getting down to lower levels and relying on something as a minimum deterrent, then counterforce is not the game. If one were talking about very low levels, say in the hundreds, there also would be a need to take into account the existing and potential capability of other nations' nuclear weapons. The British and French have programs at present that will bring them into the high hundreds range just with their submarine-launched MIRV missiles. The Chinese also have a few hundred. Those countries would have to be brought into the negotiations at some stage if the United States and the Soviet Union were to be moving down into the low thousands or below.

QUESTION: What do you think has been the relationship through the last 40 years between these massive arsenals of nuclear weapons and the actual design and conduct of foreign affairs?

MR. GARTHOFF: I think we would have seen essentially the same history even if nuclear stockpiles had been much smaller. Let's just suppose, for example, that uranium had been a much rarer element and that you had had some natural limit that would have kept us to a few hundred weapons each. It would have been the same thing.

The only historical experience that one can directly point to is the Cuban missile crisis, when the United States had an overwhelming superiority. We had about 5,000 weapons on alert, not counting re-use of bombers and not counting aircraft carriers or forward-based tactical aircraft. The Soviet Union had 200 or 300 nuclear weapons, counting everything that they could conceivably deploy; that is, some medium bombers on one-way missions and submarines with short-range missiles. The ratio of forces was something like 17 to 1 in our favor, but we were unable to exploit this advantage. If those figures had been much closer to parity or at higher levels, there would still have been concern by the President about not letting the situation develop into war. If even a few nuclear weapons were to hit one's own territory, it would be no great consolation being able to destroy the enemy's society. Of course, no one was thinking in terms of starting a nuclear war or any kind of war between the United States and the Soviet Union. The concerns were that if we were to bomb or invade Cuba, each side might then have begun an escalating series of responses. If the Soviets had then engaged in a countermove elsewhere, there was the danger of the situation getting out of control and leading to a war. That cast a very heavy shadow. It wouldn't have made any difference to President Kennedy's thinking if he had had 34-to-1 or 2-to-1 instead of 17-to-1 superiority. Nor would it have made any difference in what Khrushchev did if Soviet strategic forces had been at parity with ours at that time.

QUESTION: What are your thoughts on controlling nuclear proliferation?

MR. GARTHOFF: That is certainly coming to be recognized as one of the major problems of the post-Cold War era. One of the disadvantages of the nations of the world no longer being divided in their allegiances between the two superpowers is that we also have less influence over other countries. Granted, we were not always able to exercise that influence in controlling proliferation in the past, but at the very least the proliferation problem remains serious and may be getting worse.

The experience in the war with Iraq has brought this lesson home clearly in a way that it hadn't before. We had seriously underestimated the scope of Saddam Hussein's nuclear weapons program. Subsequent discoveries have led us to reassess the Iranian and North Korean nuclear programs, among others.

Fortunately, a number of countries have been recently moving toward acceptance of the Non-Proliferation Treaty and toward the abandonment of their own weapons programs. China is now expected to sign the Non-Proliferation Treaty; France is doing so; and Argentina and Brazil have agreed between themselves to call off any efforts toward nuclear weapons programs, and so has South Africa. I think these are all very encouraging.

Of course, Iraq is a special case since we have something of a handle on the situation at this time, but Iran and Libya could conceivably become problems. The fact that Israel is an undeclared nuclear power is an important element in the situation in the Near East. Pakistan and India are both very close to building nuclear weapons, if they don't already have them. North Korea is perhaps most politically unpredictable. I think those are the most serious cases.

There is also concern about the spread of missile technology and of chemical and biological technology that could be used for weapons. The possibility of expanding numbers of mass-destruction weapons is very serious and must be dealt with in a number of ways. One of these ways is through broad international instruments like the Non-Proliferation Treaty and a nuclear test ban. It is also necessary, however, to deal with the security concerns of individual countries. Obviously the political-military rivalry between India and Pakistan would remain, regardless of what the United States or the Soviet Union or the rest of the world did in terms of new treaties. There is a need to deal with the problem on a number of levels and through a range of political actions.

NARRATOR: When one reads Dr. Garthoff's book, one realizes there is so much about nuclear technology that we haven't absorbed. We have come to the end of the hour, even though there are many more things that would be exciting and instructive to hear from Ambassador Garthoff. On behalf of all of you, I would like to thank him very much.

II.

THE STORY
OF AN ADMINISTRATION
AND
ARMS CONTROL

CHAPTER FOUR

The Reagan Administration*

DON OBERDORFER

NARRATOR: Mr. Oberdorfer was born, grew up, and went to high school in Atlanta, Georgia. He is a graduate of Princeton University. His first position in journalism was with the *Charlotte Observer* in 1955. In the late 1960s he began working for the *Washington Post*. Mr. Oberdorfer's career has been highly productive and has earned him considerable renown.

His book, *The Turn: From the Cold War to a New Era*, is already considered one of the major works in the field of Soviet-American relations. It is especially important because, in contrast to many other books, it suggests that there were actors who played decisive roles other than Reagan and Gorbachev. He is also author of *Tet!*, considered by many to be the authoritative work on that aspect of the Vietnam War.

Beyond that, he is someone who has a wide readership, particularly among scholars searching for leads to problems in their own work. His high reputation is well deserved. We are delighted that he could talk about Soviet-American relations, especially regarding the Reagan administration.

---

*Presented in a Forum at the Miller Center of Public Affairs on 2 December 1991.

MR. OBERDORFER: I would like to begin by taking you back eight years to the fall of 1983, which in historical terms is like the blink of an eye. At that time the United States and the Soviet Union were locked in an intense confrontation that alarmed some of our leading scholars. George Kennan, perhaps the most eminent scholar of Soviet-American relations, wrote that the only way to interpret the behavior of the two countries was that they were headed inexorably toward war.

In September 1983 the Soviet Union shot down an unarmed Korean airliner, flight KAL 007, which had ventured into its airspace. Later in the fall, the United States deployed medium-range missiles in Western Europe for the first time under a NATO agreement, and the Soviet Union reacted by walking out of the Geneva arms talks. Yuri Andropov, who was then the head of the Communist party and leader of the Soviet Union, issued a statement that anyone who thought there was any possibility of improved relations between the two countries while the Reagan administration was in power should be disabused of that notion. In early November of that year, the Soviet Union alerted its KGB intelligence stations around the world to gather on an urgent basis information concerning what the central headquarters in Moscow believed was an imminent United States nuclear attack on the Soviet Union.

It is hard for us now to cast our minds back just eight years to the period when the confrontation was that intense, and yet it was only a short time ago. My book basically describes how these two nations managed to engage each other and ease tensions, thus ending the Cold War.

The Cold War was based on mutual fear, and neither side's fear of the other was entirely misplaced. What the conflict really represented was not just a collision of historical forces, but a great misunderstanding between the two sides. I tried to tell the story of how we emerged from that period of intense confrontation and angst to reach the transformed world today. I covered these events for the *Washington Post*. My most important assignment since 1978 was to follow Soviet-American relations.

When I came back from Japan in 1975 after covering that country for three years, I joined the diplomatic beat. My senior colleague was Murrey Marder. I was doing the Middle East and Murrey was doing Soviet and East-West matters. In the middle of 1978 he took a leave of absence. I asked him whether I should stay with the Middle East or take over East-West and Soviet affairs. He said I should cover the Soviet Union. I asked why, and he said because that was "the only country that could kill us in the short run." Such a thought tends to concentrate the mind. They have 27,000 nuclear warheads in that country even today.

I won't recount the story of how the leaders of the two nations began to interrelate, which is the only way to accomplish a major change in relationships between hostile governments. The most interesting events followed the death of Yuri Andropov in early 1984 and the ascension to power of Konstantin Chernenko. He was an apparatchik assistant of Brezhnev and was so sick from emphysema that he couldn't even raise his arm high enough to salute at the parade when he was inaugurated. He only lasted a year. Then in March 1985 came Gorbachev, who was a new kind of leader.

In the fall of 1985 Gorbachev and Reagan had their first meeting at Geneva. One year later they met again in Reykjavík, Iceland, which was perhaps the most dramatic and spectacular Soviet-American meeting since Yalta in 1945 or the Kennedy-Khrushchev meeting of 1961. The two leaders, their foreign ministers Shultz and Shevardnadze, two interpreters, and two notetakers sat alone in a room much smaller than this around a dining room-sized table. They bargained about the entire stock of U.S. and Soviet ballistic missiles, which were, in effect, the foundations of their national power. At the end, they even talked about eliminating all nuclear weapons from their respective arsenals. It was an incredible leap into the future and seemed utterly impractical at the time. It seems a little less bizarre now, since President Bush and Mr. Gorbachev are talking about large cuts in U.S. and Soviet weapons for the first time since those days in October 1986.

Next came the Washington summit in 1987 when Gorbachev came to Washington, Reagan's trip to Moscow's Red Square in 1988, and Gorbachev's surprise trip to the United Nations in December 1988 just before President Reagan left office. At the

United Nations, Gorbachev announced first that the Soviet Union had taken a new path and was looking at its relations with the rest of the world in a new way. Second, Gorbachev said the Soviets were going to unilaterally cut half a million men from their armed forces.

By the end of the Reagan administration in January 1989, it was clear that the two nations were on a new path that would have an impact on strategic relationships throughout the world. I decided to write this book in the summer and early fall of 1988 after Reagan visited Red Square. It struck me that this was a momentous event and that I would never again witness anything as important as what I had seen take place in the past three or four years between these two countries. I wanted to go beyond what I knew at the time in order to learn more and record what I could for history.

There are many metaphors for the job of journalist, but the one that I like best has to do with icebergs. What we do is report the tip of the iceberg, that which is visible today. Our duty as journalists is to get as far down below the waterline as we can by getting to people who will tell us the things we don't see.

We know perfectly well that we know only a small part of the story. We never admit as much in public because it wouldn't help our credibility among readers, but any good journalist knows perfectly well that this is true.

With my book on the Tet offensive and with *The Turn*, I learned a great deal by returning a year or two later to see the people who were involved, especially those who were no longer in office and thus freer to talk. This semidetached perspective adds a vital dimension that news chronicles lack.

Philip Graham, who was the publisher of the *Washington Post* at one time, was quoted as having said, "Journalism is the first rough draft of history," which is a nice way to think about it. What I call "contemporary history" is the second rough draft. That involves filling in the gaps between the facts you already know in order to have a better understanding and broader perspective.

I had intended originally to end my book at the close of the Reagan administration. It had a wonderful ending: Secretary Shultz and his wife were watching the inauguration of Bush on television because they had not been invited. They then boarded a plane and flew to California.

The events of 1989 were so spectacular, however, especially the demise of the Communist governments in Eastern Europe, that I just couldn't leave them out. So, I decided to cover such key events as the reunification of Germany and finally ended the book with the Washington summit of June 1990. Many people have asked me why I ended it then, and the real answer is because that is when I took my prearranged leave of absence and started to write the book.

By then the great turning point in Soviet-American relations had clearly taken place. Even so, I did not foresee, and don't know anybody who foresaw, the events of August 1991 and their earth-shaking consequences for Soviet affairs and relations between the major countries of the world. That is another story for someone else's book. My book concerns how these two big "ships" managed a complete turn in course.

Who and what are responsible for what happened? All of you know, and I'm sure some know far better than I, that there has been an age-old argument among historians about whether the main movers of historical events are underlying trends or individual people. Clearly, both play a part, and in this case the underlying trends were very important. Among them perhaps the most important was the development of a global economy, which is the driving force behind most of the advanced national economies today. Soviet leaders knew that unless they could change their system and become a part of the global market, they would be left far behind.

I remember a conversation I had in Moscow in early 1984, before Gorbachev came in, with a man named Fyodor Burlatsky, who had recently been in Washington. He had been a speech writer and aide to Khrushchev, and knew Gorbachev and Andropov as well. In the middle of our conversation he said to me, "Do you know the country that bothers us most, and it isn't you [meaning the United States]?" I said, "No, which one is it?" He said it was Japan. I asked why they were worried about Japan, and he said, "Because they are in the forefront of the third industrial revolution, and we are nowhere." He was referring to the high-technology computer age. Soviet leadership, with some help from outsiders such as former Secretary of State Shultz, began to understand that they were nowhere and that they had to change.

A second factor that people forget is the demographic change that had taken place in the Soviet Union. On the eve of World War II the population of the country was two-thirds rural, and less than 10 percent had even a high school education. It was a country consisting mainly of peasants, plus some urban workers and a small elite on top.

By the 1980s the country was two-thirds urbanized, about the same as Western Europe. The standards of education, while still lacking, had been almost revolutionarily improved. A very high percentage of the population had finished high school and many had university degrees. Even though the country was still ruled by a Byzantine system with a very small group of people at the top, many more people were becoming aware of what was going on in the outside world and within their own country, and there was a tremendous demand for change.

The third big factor was that the Soviet and American leaders understood at least implicitly that in the nuclear age it was simply too dangerous for two such heavily armed nations to be at loggerheads with one another. Something had to be done to defuse this danger or else sooner or later there would be a clash that would be the end of both countries.

Having outlined these key underlying factors, we turn to the aspect of how the individual people interacted. One almost has to start with Mikhail Gorbachev. For all of his shortcomings, failings, indecision, and lack of understanding of economics and other factors, I think he will be regarded as one of the great figures of the 20th century. I don't have much doubt about it. While he could not foresee the ultimate end of the process that he began in his country, it was a matter of tremendous historical importance.

Kennan once remarked in the late 1980s that he and other experts on Soviet affairs were mystified that a person from a provincial area in the northern Caucasus like Gorbachev could possess such political ability and a grasp of skills and ideas. It is still a very good question. Several correspondents who have recently been in Moscow are writing books about Gorbachev's life and the background of his policies, and we will probably learn more about this in the next year or two.

Eduard Shevardnadze was another remarkable person who was probably responsible for more of these foreign policy changes than we yet know. Shevardnadze had been the Communist party boss of Georgia. He had not a single day's experience in diplomacy or democracy when his friend Gorbachev picked him to be foreign minister in the summer of 1985. Yet he became a respected diplomat and a "small d" democrat. Some of the things that he said within the Soviet Union are absolutely amazing for someone who had been an orthodox Communist figure. There had never before been a Soviet foreign minister who had gained such a high degree of trust and confidence as Shevardnadze developed with George Shultz, James Baker, and other world leaders. This was an amazing change, and he remains a major historical figure.

President Reagan is also a leading figure in all this. In the course of writing this book, I learned some things about Reagan I didn't know before that helped to explain some of what happened. In the first place, I learned that throughout his term Reagan was much more interested in engaging the Russians in a dialogue than I had thought as a reporter. In public, Reagan was condemning the Soviets in the harshest of terms, such as "evil empire," and was the most anti-Communist leader that we ever had. But that was all on the surface; that was the tip of the iceberg.

What we didn't know was a fact concealed "beneath the iceberg" in large part: at the same time he berated the Soviets, Reagan was very eager to engage them. Even when he was condemning them with his harshest rhetoric in early 1983, he was asking Shultz to do what he could to become engaged with the Soviets because Reagan wanted to go to Moscow. He always believed if he could just get a Soviet leader into a room for a private talk, he could convince him.

Secondly, Reagan had an absolute abhorrence of nuclear weapons. He often said this, but most of us didn't take it very seriously. The image of him as a cowboy riding out of the West, chopping his wood and that sort of thing made us discount his repeated statements that he wanted to rid the world of nuclear weapons. Our perceptions changed after Reykjavík, when Reagan put the whole pile of nuclear weapons on the bargaining table. The "Star Wars" program, or SDI, was another manifestation of Reagan's desire to stop nuclear weapons.

I think Reagan knew in general terms what he wanted to do with the Soviets, but he didn't know how to go about doing it. He tried writing some personal letters to Soviet leaders, but it didn't have much impact.

The person who helped Reagan accomplish what he did accomplish in relations with the Soviets was George Shultz, who is another remarkable person. Shultz is an academic economist who was appointed to high political office. He is a very persistent, dogged person. However, he did not have, in my opinion, the diplomatic brilliance of Henry Kissinger. He is not a world strategic thinker, but he had a clear conception of where he wanted to go with the Soviets.

His persistence was very important in an administration that was greatly divided over Soviet affairs, where various factions were pulling and hauling. Everything that the United States did in this area was controversial in Washington. Even though the President knew in general what he wanted to do, Shultz was extremely important in getting something done. There were many other actors in the story, as is always true of diplomatic situations—some of them by virtue of their position and others by accident, but these four men were the most important.

Where does it all end? What happens now, after the August coup, the demise of the Soviet Communist party, and the very likely breakup of the Soviet Union into several constituent parts? How does the world deal with this? How can we even think about a world in which the Soviet Union, which has been the leader of one of the two great blocs in the world since the middle of the 1940s, is no longer an international player, and even Russia is not much of an international player?

We are just beginning to try to grapple with and think through all these questions. As a reporter, I find myself surprised almost every day and uncertain about what might happen next. This is essentially the reason that I decided to devote a six-month leave of absence from the newspaper to try to put together the story of this great turning point. I felt everything had happened so fast that I could hardly grasp it myself. If I can't grasp it, certainly the people who are not following it that closely and just reading the daily headlines are going to have trouble figuring out what happened. Somebody else will have to write another book on the period from shortly before the August coup to the present.

NARRATOR: There is a mystery about Shultz and his background in diplomacy, isn't there? Henry Kissinger said that when he had to give speeches on such economic topics as the International Monetary Fund or the balance of payments, he would get somebody to brief him. They would pound the stuff into his head and he would give a credible speech, but he said, "I never felt it in my gut."

Kissinger once said that the one person in the United States that he knew who was qualified to be president was George Shultz. That was before Bush came in, and perhaps even before Reagan. But he then went on to say that George Shultz in diplomacy was like he (Kissinger) was in economics. He said he could not remember a conversation where George Shultz had discussed any issue in diplomacy with him for more than a sentence or two. Concerning diplomacy, Kissinger said he simply felt that George Shultz "didn't feel it in his gut," just as he didn't feel economics in his gut. Yet, Shultz is the man who accomplished this diplomatic miracle. How do you account for it?

MR. OBERDORFER: As I said, I don't think Shultz was any great strategic thinker. In Kissingerian terms, he was not creating some intricate balance of power in the world, but he knew what his objective was—namely, a much healthier, more sensible relationship with reduced tension between the two superpowers.

Shultz knew that to attain this objective he had to develop a relationship of confidence and trust among his own people and with the Soviet negotiators. He was a tough bargainer. He's a tough guy in many respects and is no pushover for anybody.

He began to believe through personal contacts that these new Soviet leaders were serious about what they said they were trying to do, while much of Washington did not yet believe it. For example, in September 1987 Shevardnadze came to Washington and asked for a private meeting with Shultz. Shultz took him and his interpreter into the back office of the secretary of state, not his ceremonial office, but the one that they really use for their work. Shevardnadze told him, "We are getting out of Afghanistan, and we are probably going to be out by the time your administration is over. We need your help."

Shultz took this to heart. However, after the meeting they went to a conference room in the secretary's suite where the two delegations were discussing regional issues, and the Soviet position on Afghanistan was just the same as it has always been. It was total nonsense! Shultz was saying, "Why am I hearing this? What is going on here?" But he believed that Shevardnadze was serious and that the rest of this stuff was just for show; it was a smoke screen. He said nothing about it publicly, but he urged other U.S. government officials to take this seriously.

The CIA, other intelligence agencies, and most other people in the U.S. government who were familiar with Afghanistan didn't believe it. The Soviet Union had never retreated under fire—why should they do so now?

The point is that Shultz had a rather deep interaction with people who in their own way were revolutionary figures in the Soviet Union. He had enough confidence in what they were telling him not only to believe it but to try to act on it.

What is diplomacy all about, anyway? Some of the great diplomats in history have been strategic thinkers, while others have been front-line doers. I don't know whether James Baker will end up being regarded as a great diplomat or not, but his role is that of a negotiator. Shultz was a negotiator in a different kind of way.

Let me tell one other story about Shultz, because I find it so interesting. Most of what I know about Shultz's negotiations, by the way, I did not learn while I was covering the story. He wouldn't talk about sensitive matters with me or other reporters; he wouldn't breathe a word of what he was saying to Reagan or what Reagan was saying to him. He abhorred talking about any internal administration discussions. It was only after he had left office and agreed to help me with my book that he began to tell me what really happened.

I had 13 long interviews with Shultz, amounting to 24 hours of taped conversations. Someone asked me recently, "Who were your sources in the Soviet Union, Sovietologists?" To the contrary, I used to be glad if I could see the second assistant door opener of the central committee, much less a real professor. I was fortunate that Shevardnadze gave to me the only book interview that he gave during his first term as foreign minister. He also persuaded his subordinates to see me. My other sources included five deputy foreign ministers and three members of the Politburo; I spent four-and-a-half hours in the Kremlin with Marshal Akhromeyev, the chief military adviser to Gorbachev.

The story about Shultz is that in October he went to Moscow on one of his negotiating trips. It had been agreed the month before when Shevardnadze was in the United States that on this occasion Gorbachev would set the date for the next summit meeting to take place in Washington.

Gorbachev and Shultz had a rather contentious meeting, and Gorbachev refused to set the date at the end of the meeting. Besides being an economist and academic dean, Shultz had a great deal of experience in labor-management negotiations and was good at sizing up people on the other side of the table. He was very shrewd on this.

As they left this puzzling meeting, Shultz said to the small group who participated with him in the meeting, "There is something different about Gorbachev. I noticed it in the first moments of that meeting. Gorbachev has always reminded me of a line in a poem by Carl Sandburg." Shultz was referring to "Chicago," the famous Sandburg poem about an ignorant fighter who had never lost a battle. He said, "Gorbachev has always reminded me of this fighter who had never been hit. But only a few minutes after our discussions began I said to myself, 'This fighter has been hit, but I don't know who hit him.'"

Ten days later they found out that the day before this meeting with Shultz there had been a big meeting of the Communist party Central Committee. For the first time, Boris Yeltsin got up and attacked both Gorbachev and Ligachev, who was on the other side ideologically. Gorbachev thereafter became a little vulnerable in his own political speech.

I know that Shultz is not making this up because I have interviewed the people who were there with him. Still, it seems incredible that he could sit at this table, observe Gorbachev's manner, and say, "This fighter has been hit." Shultz had a keen feel for the way people act on the other side of the table.

Many of you probably knew Bryce Harlow, a key aide to Republican presidents. Shultz told the story of going to see Bryce Harlow soon after arriving in Washington as secretary of labor for Nixon's first administration. Harlow said to him, "Trust is the coin of the realm." If you are going to deal with people, you have to trust them. There were people whom Shultz came not to trust, but they weren't around too long in his State Department.

QUESTION: I wonder if we were just plain lucky to have had people like Shultz and Reagan running this country at a crucial time, and whether we could therefore in the reverse luck of the draw once again find ourselves on the brink of apocalypse as you described in 1983? Do we have some sort of mystique that enables us to muddle through with pygmies in charge instead of giants?

MR. OBERDORFER: I don't want to be misunderstood in my feelings for Reagan. I'm no fan of President Reagan in many respects. I think what he did with the economy was a disaster, and allowing the United States to go so deeply into debt was absolutely irresponsible. There were many other Reagan policies with which I disagreed.

In this particular field, however, in a funny way Reagan was the right man at the right time. Because he was the most right-wing president we had ever had, it was easier for him to make an accommodation with the Soviet Union than a centrist or liberal president. Otherwise, there would have been someone like Ronald Reagan on his right screaming that we were giving up everything to the Russians. On balance, I do think he did a fine job in the way things came out with the Soviet Union.

I think implied in your question is whether we might go back to confrontation with the Soviet Union. I think the answer is definitely no, it will never be the same. True, there could be great dangers for the rest of the world in the situation in the Soviet Union because of their nuclear weapons and other things. There will indeed be many unforeseeable consequences of the collapse of one of the great empires of our time. But the Soviet Union will not revert to leading a bloc of nations ideologically committed to confrontation with the West, at least in the foreseeable future. There no longer exists the comprehensive threat to peace that we perceived communism posed.

Regarding our current leadership, up until a month ago I would have said that in foreign policy Bush was about as good a president as we could get. He knows his stuff, is interested, and takes a clear position on foreign affairs. The administration, however, has suddenly plunged into some kind of crisis within itself as to what it is going to do.

I was absolutely stunned that the members of Congress who proposed an appropriation bill to assist the Soviet Union in dismantling their nuclear weapons could not get any expression of support from Bush. He just took a dive on the whole issue. I wrote about this recently in the *Washington Post* Outlook section. I don't know what Bush is likely to do now. I fear that we are going to have another year, or perhaps five years, of immobility because the administration is so stunned by the perception of economic reversals in the United States.

QUESTION: Would the failure of the Russian military to act to fill a vacuum be due merely to the failure of the economic and industrial system in Russia? Why haven't they done something?

MR. OBERDORFER: There was no consensus in the Russian military about what to do, and besides, there is not much of a history in that country of the military playing a decisive role in politics. Some military leaders backed the August coup; others did not. I think that if the economic circumstances continue to deteriorate and the people of the Soviet Union face ever-bleaker prospects as the state breaks up, there is a great danger that some other force, military or nonmilitary, will try to assert control and say to the people of the country, "We offer a way out." It is hard to imagine a collapse of authority taking place without somebody trying to provide some kind of leadership. The present Soviet military leaders, however, definitely disapprove of any attempted coup or other such use of its power for political ends. Whether that disinclination will continue to prevail in the future, I don't know.

QUESTION: You began by speaking of the crisis mood of 1983. Beginning in January 1984, the tone of Reagan's public statements and speeches changed completely. There was a very sudden shift in emphasis toward accommodation and summit meetings. I wonder if you have any knowledge as to what may lie behind that shift.

MR. OBERDORFER: I have a good deal of knowledge about it. I won't go into the details that are set forth in the book, but starting in the spring of 1983 some of the political advisers around Reagan looked forward to the 1984 election year and warned that a confrontational posture with the Soviets might cost votes. Moreover, Reagan had always thought that the United States should first build up the military and then negotiate from a position of strength, and there was a sense that he had done that. In the first two years the military buildup had proceeded, and it was now time to begin negotiations.

A person could make that claim in retrospect, but you would have to question whether they were saying the same thing at the time. To me, the most interesting and compelling evidence came from Jack Matlock, who at the time was the U.S. ambassador to one of the Eastern European countries and later became ambassador to the Soviet Union. He was called back to Washington and asked by Bill Clark and Bud McFarlane to take the job of head of Soviet and European affairs on the National Security Council staff. They told him that this was an important post because the military buildup had now gone far enough, so it was time to get down to negotiations.

Reagan actually tried to begin this in August 1983 when he wrote a letter to Andropov along these lines, but shortly thereafter the Soviets shot down Korean Airlines flight 007. That fall there was horrible tension over this incident, the missile situation, and everything else, and it wasn't until early 1984 that he was able to reverse the diplomatic trend. You are correct in saying that there was a definite shift in the wind, not only in Washington but in Moscow as well.

76

QUESTION: You have given us a wonderful overview of the long-term trends. You have also commented on the military buildup under the Reagan administration. Was our military buildup designed to spend the Soviets into the ground? Has this tremendous military buildup contributed to what is happening in the Soviet Union today?

MR. OBERDORFER: This has become a very controversial issue. Many Americans did not approve of the military buildup and thought it was a waste of money. There was particularly intense political argument over the SDI question.

My conclusion is that the military buildup, especially the SDI and high-technology parts of the buildup, was a contributing factor to the Soviet decision to take a new road. I don't think it was the central factor. I think the greater factors were things that I have already mentioned—the economic circumstances, the social and demographic changes within the Soviet Union, and the sense that the nuclear arms race was just too dangerous. The last thing they thought they could afford was a high-technology arms race with the United States.

What Gorbachev did at Geneva and especially at Reykjavík was to try at all costs to get Reagan to stop the SDI program. That was his central objective. I think the Soviets feared this new type of competition that would have cost them dearly and which they could not possibly have won. So I do think it was a factor. In the future, some person who has more erudition than I will have to figure out how much of a factor.

QUESTION: Now that Gorbachev's influence has diminished and there are new players in the field such as Yeltsin and other leaders of the various republics—for example, the Ukraine—what happens to the hot line between Washington and Moscow?

MR. OBERDORFER: At the moment it goes from the Pentagon to the headquarters of the Soviet military. I think we still need it. In fact, I think we need more hot lines to the Ukraine, Kazakhstan, and other republics.

You probably read in the paper that the *Bulletin of the Atomic Scientists* a few days ago moved their minute hand of the "doomsday clock" back as far as it has ever been because of what has happened. I might have been inclined to move it a little in the other direction because I think the idea of 27,000 nuclear warheads in a country that is coming apart is not one that is particularly comforting. It is hard to believe that this chaotic situation is not going to jeopardize central control over these horrible weapons.

I don't know how many of you have ever been to Hiroshima or Nagasaki, but I visited these cities while I was a correspondent in Japan. The museums there show the destruction caused by one nuclear weapon that is merely a toy compared to today's weapons. The thought of these weapons being out of control just terrifies me. We need to keep this hot line and have some other smaller branch hot lines.

QUESTION: Would you comment on the personal and working relationship between Shevardnadze and Gorbachev? How well do they work together?

MR. OBERDORFER: In the period I covered they worked very closely together. What I don't know is to what extent the initiative for various proposals came from Shevardnadze. We know, for example, that Shevardnadze was chairman of the Politburo Commission on Afghanistan. What we don't know is how that commission worked. We know it decided that the Soviet Union should get out of Afghanistan, but how did it reach that decision? Gorbachev may have developed the strategy for withdrawing from Afghanistan, or he may have said to his friend Shevardnadze, "We know where we want to go. You make it happen!" We don't know.

In December 1990 Shevardnadze came to feel that Gorbachev was not backing him up. Gorbachev had turned to the right that fall, and there were increasing attacks on Shevardnadze. Shevardnadze felt that Gorbachev was letting this happen and not standing up as he should, and Shevardnadze resigned in that dramatic speech where he said there was a possibility of dictatorship in the country.

He didn't tell Gorbachev what he was going to do ahead of time. He had tried to resign once before, but Gorbachev talked him out of it. From then on through most of this year he was an outside critic, a friendly critic in some respects, but speaking rather openly of Gorbachev's failings. About two weeks ago Gorbachev convinced him to come back.

QUESTION: Wasn't it a surprise that Gorbachev wanted him to come back?

MR. OBERDORFER: It was not a surprise to me that he wanted him. It was a surprise to me that Shevardnadze agreed.

COMMENT: He didn't have to work with Gorbachev. He could have continued in some other way.

MR. OBERDORFER: He was head of an institute, but I think he came to realize his institute didn't have much impact on things. It was at a time of revolutionary change in his country, and I imagine it was hard for him to sit on the sidelines. Gorbachev probably appealed to him by saying (this is a guess), "Look, Eduard, you know this is the moment when the country is either going to continue or everything is going to fall apart. I need you."

It is interesting that his first major act as foreign minister was to announce that he would visit the capitals of all 12 republics. He understands where the problem is and where the priorities are. They are not in Paris, London, or Washington, but rather in the Ukraine, Kazakhstan, Armenia, Azerbaijan, and the other republics. He is a good politician, so if anyone has a chance to try to work constructively with these national groups, it is Shevardnadze. Whether he will be able to succeed, I don't know; I doubt it.

QUESTION: Do you feel that Gorbachev will be out of office eventually?

MR. OBERDORFER: Whether it is by resignation or some other method such as ouster, I don't expect him to be around by this time next year.

79

QUESTION: Do you think there will be a replacement for him, a hard-line person?

MR. OBERDORFER: No one quite knows what the new system will be like or what kind of central authority there will be. Very shortly the Russian Republic is going to take over paying all the bills (to the extent they are paid at all) for the main central governmental agencies. That will give them control over those agencies. So, what will be left for a central coordinating authority to do? It is going to be a little like the Articles of Confederation period in early U.S. history. There will be the need for some coordinating mechanism. Who can do it? What are the ground rules going to be and under what circumstances? Gorbachev clearly has the greatest talent for this kind of thing, but will he be willing to remain in what is mostly a figurehead role over a long period of time? I doubt he would play second fiddle to Yeltsin, with whom he doesn't really get along.

COMMENT: It is almost an embarrassment to him.

MR. OBERDORFER: Yes, but to his credit, he is not thinking in terms of pride or embarrassment. He keeps seeing possibilities to salvage the situation that no one else seems to see. Maybe that is good.

QUESTION: On the nuclear side, did I hear you correctly when you spoke of events in 1983? I remember the crisis over the Korean airliner, and things were tense, but I don't think there was any notion in this country that Russia thought we were about to launch a nuclear attack. That is sort of a misconception.

MR. OBERDORFER: We didn't know it then. We know it now only because the KGB station chief in London, a man named Oleg Gordievsky, was secretly working for Western intelligence. When he defected several years later, his story became public. The Soviets actually alerted some of their nuclear-capable aircraft in Eastern Europe to be ready to take off. It was frightening! The government knew it within a few weeks because of Gordievsky.

Reagan alludes to it vaguely in his memoirs; other people were much more conscious of it, and the CIA did some evaluations on whether there was a serious danger. Reagan said to McFarlane, "You know, I can't believe that these people really think we are going to attack them. Why would they think that?"

But some people in Moscow evidently did. In the next year or two as the Soviet archives are opened and people become more willing to talk, we will probably learn more about why they thought this, and what really happened in that period. It is rather gripping that they thought they were about to be attacked.

QUESTION: If the Soviet Union is calling back Shevardnadze, who negotiated so well for them, why aren't we calling back our secretary of state who negotiated so well with him?

MR. OBERDORFER: We have a secretary of state who negotiated pretty well with Shevardnadze in the first two years of the Bush administration. Baker had and continues to have an excellent relationship with Shevardnadze.

COMMENT: But it was George Shultz who thought through the plan that still must be carried out successfully.

MR. OBERDORFER: That is true. I have a favorite phrase about journalism that applies in a certain way to the field of government. I have always been fond of quoting the dedication to a book written by A. J. Liebling, who was the great critic of the press for the *New Yorker* years ago. His dedication said, "For a school for publishers, without which no school for journalists can have any meaning."

In the end, it is the president who determines the foreign policy of the United States; Congress and the State Department play a subordinate role. The president must be comfortable with his secretary of state and other chief negotiators. He has to have the relationship with them that makes it possible for them to go out and work on his behalf.

In this particular case, George Bush and James Baker probably have the closest relationship that any president and secretary of state have had since the beginning of the republic. Jim Baker was

Bush's campaign manager for the Senate race in Texas, for president in 1980 when he was beaten by Reagan, and in 1988. They are very close friends.

We also have a different arrangement for running foreign policy today. In most cases since World War II, the secretary of state has been an expert on foreign affairs, or becomes so if he isn't already when he takes office; the president is usually an expert on politics.

The secretary of state, secretary of defense, and national security adviser meet with the president and explain to him the main considerations of a given problem in an overseas area. Normally the president follows their recommendations.

In this case, the President is an expert on foreign policy. He has a good idea of what he wants to do. He knows all these places since he has traveled almost everywhere in the world. He probably knows half of the senior-level diplomats. The secretary of state happens to be an expert on American politics. Bush gives more specific direction to diplomacy than any president has since Nixon. The secretary of state thus serves as the chief negotiator. He's an adviser to a degree, but I think less so than has usually been the case.

Every president needs an organization and staffing that suits his own personality and circumstances. Just because George Shultz was successful under Ronald Reagan doesn't mean he would be that successful under Mr. Bush.

NARRATOR: Did Shultz ever explain why he thought he wasn't invited to the inauguration? That seems to go one step beyond simply not conferring with the former secretary of state during a transition to a new administration. Was there a Bush-Shultz relationship that figured into your study in any way?

MR. OBERDORFER: I asked him this and he said he did not know why he was not invited. Bush's relationship with Shultz for the most part was pretty good because the two men stood on the same side of most issues.

They did have a falling out, however, over the Iran-contra affair. Bush felt that Shultz was not being loyal enough to the

President, and was protecting his own position. Shultz felt that Reagan and the administration were tremendously mistaken in trying to do what they were doing. He had been opposed to it from the beginning, and he said so rather outspokenly. But I don't believe that really accounts for it because people in politics always disagree about something. They are all grownups.

I think the Bush administration basically wanted to show it wasn't just a third Reagan administration. They wanted to get the old guys out of town as fast as possible. It may have just been an oversight, but I don't know. It was rather bizarre that a man who had served six-and-a-half years as secretary of state should be in effect shunted out of town. This was the longest that anyone had served as secretary of state in the postwar period except for Dean Rusk and John Foster Dulles.

QUESTION: Given the momentum of events in the latter part of 1988 and the presumed involvement of Bush's people who served under Reagan, why did it seem to take the new administration so long to get organized and march off in a new direction or to respond to the initiatives of the Soviet Union?

MR. OBERDORFER: Bush was very cautious and felt that the Reagan administration had gone too far to fast toward the end of its term. He was appalled by the rashness of the proposals at Reykjavík. He didn't like the political aura that developed between the United States and the Soviet Union. Let's not forget, he didn't have the same right-wing credentials that Reagan had and was vulnerable to attack from that direction. So, in the beginning of his term he was extremely cautious, and the administration was strangely slow in organizing itself. One would think it would be easy since they were taking over from another Republican administration, but it didn't work that way.

It was only in the summer of 1989, when Baker really began to engage with Shevardnadze and Gorbachev and things began to change in Eastern Europe, that the administration got itself together. I believe it took so long mainly because of two factors: first, Bush's caution, and second, the administration's slowness in appointing people to important positions.

III.

VIEWS
FROM THE
PRESIDENT'S NEGOTIATORS

CHAPTER FIVE

Organizing Arms Control in the U.S. Government*

AMBASSADOR MAYNARD GLITMAN

NARRATOR: Few diplomats have had Ambassador Maynard Glitman's intensive exposure to the problems of negotiating arms control. In 1976, he was engaged in INF (intermediate-range nuclear force) negotiations and continued to the end of the negotiations and ratification. He joined the Foreign Service of the State Department in 1956, first as an economist, then as economic officer of the U.S. Embassy in Ottawa, next as a member of the U.S. delegation to the United Nations General Assembly, and thereafter as a member of the National Security Council staff.

He became a political officer at the American Embassy in Paris and then director of the Office of International Trade at the Department of State. He was named Deputy Assistant Secretary for International Trade then Deputy Assistant Secretary of Defense for Europe and NATO. He also became the United States Deputy Permanent Representative to NATO.

---

*Presented in a Forum at the Miller Center of Public Affairs on 20 September 1991. Ambassador Glitman's views and opinions are solely his own and do not necessarily represent those of the United States Government.

Then came his involvement in arms negotiations. In the INF negotiations, he was Ambassador and Deputy Chief of the U.S. Delegation with the Arms Control and Disarmament Agency (ACDA) in Geneva from 1981 to 1984. Following that, he was appointed, successively, Ambassador and U.S. Representative to the Mutual Balanced Force Reductions (MBFR) negotiations in Vienna, and from 1985 to 1988, Ambassador and Chief Negotiator of the Intermediate-range Nuclear Force negotiations in Geneva, which we all watched with such hope, pride, and pleasure when it completed its work successfully. Ambassador Glitman initialed the treaty on behalf of the United States.

He served in the U.S. Army. He was a recipient of two Public Service Medals of the U.S. Department of Defense and three Presidential Award Medals.

We look forward to a lively discussion on some of the questions we have addressed to him.

MR. GLITMAN: I thought I would answer the questions given me in advance, and then I would be happy to answer your questions. First, how did the government organize itself for arms control policy in the Reagan administration? As I watched the administration trying to deal with the subject of arms control, I developed a theory as to how an administration goes about organizing itself. The first thing decided on is who will be appointed to the positions; second, those individuals mark off their "turf"; and third comes the determination of policy.

In the case of the Reagan administration, there was a considerable delay before ACDA got organized. As a result, before they could decide on the "who" for ACDA, other parts of the government were organized and began dividing up the "turf" and setting policy. Consequently, ACDA began to lose its position simply because no one was in charge until Eugene Rostow got there. Once he arrived, it was a little hard to fight for the turf, because the others had established so much power over the issues. There was, of course, a considerable discussion of policy following that, but that sequence of events is one worth remembering.

I don't know if this way of looking at things gets into textbooks, but I have found it to hold true in general. One would have thought that as a policymaker, you would start with the issues, then go to the institutions, and finally to the personalities. That is the way one would like to see it done, but it just doesn't work that way.

There was certainly a fairly organized arrangement. We had a day-to-day backstopping group that was housed in ACDA. That group would coordinate the interagency process and get instructions to us on given issues. But, this was largely a nuts and bolts operation. There were also a number of committees, whether chaired by the State Department or Defense Department, the two of them together, or by the NSC, depending on the nature of the subject. These dealt with the larger issues.

There is a sort of natural progression of issues flowing up to the top. The effort is always to try and resolve the issue at the lowest possible level; that often doesn't work, and the issues move up to the next highest level. Sometimes there is a temptation not to bring the issues to the National Security Council or to the President, in part it is often argued, because he shouldn't be bothered with that type of question. But the practical result is that those who don't want to change a position or take an initiative are able to block progress by keeping the issue away from the President. Obviously, a way had to be developed to ensure a fair hearing. That was eventually done inside the Reagan administration via the NSC taking a leading role. Otherwise, the disagreements particularly between the State Department and the Pentagon would have resulted in stalemates.

The next question was about the role of ACDA. As I indirectly pointed out, a lot depended upon who was in charge of ACDA. I don't really like to get into personalities, but there were three ACDA directors during the time we did the negotiations. Each one approached the job slightly differently, and in each case they obviously tried to give ACDA as important a role as they possibly could. I think it was an uphill battle for the reasons that I already explained. Perhaps with different leadership the results would have been different, but I would have to be frank and say that I don't think ACDA played the key role in the INF area. It had an essential role in that they did have the job of getting out the normal instructions and so on. But if an issue really required high-level attention, the ACDA director would be only one of the people in the room, and certainly not the key player.

The next question concerns the role of the negotiators in the field. I believe we were able to make a major contribution to the process. One of the reasons for this was that everyone else had other tasks. Our work centered almost exclusively on the negotiations. As a consequence, we knew more about it than anyone else. It wasn't because we were smarter; it was just that we were concentrating on it.

But this gave us a tremendous degree of influence because our views were based on more solid information. Provided our arguments were also solid and well presented, they often carried the day and had great influence. In looking back over the course of the negotiations, my sense is, therefore, that the negotiators did have a major impact on the development of the strategy for the negotiation as well as the tactics and implementation.

The Secretary of State's role was crucial. It is not easy for the Secretary to spend a lot of time on a negotiation, but I know that George Shultz, in particular, did spend a lot of time on INF. Sometimes I felt sorry that we had to call him in, but when issues reached a crucial point where I, as the negotiator, had done as much as I could do—where we had gotten to a point where we had to raise the ante, so to speak—then we would call back and say it was time for the Secretary to intervene. Invariably he did, and always in a helpful and useful manner. I have to say that if he had not intervened and come to Geneva, Moscow, Washington, or wherever, we probably would not have been able to get through, because politically sensitive issues do arise that negotiators, while they will have an opinion and advice, simply do not have the political power base to resolve.

That is not to say negotiators cannot make smaller decisions, and I made many. For example, it's 4:00 a.m., the Treaty is scheduled for signature in 48 hours, and we have to come to closure then and there. There is no one available to approve whether I should agree to a particular time line: Should it be three, four, or five hours? So you do it, and trust that your knowledge, background, and instincts will lead you to make the best choice. On the major issues, however, you do need the Secretary.

The NSC role was also very crucial. As I pointed out, I have never seen any administration in which you had total harmony among the agencies; you can't expect that. The job of the NSC is to try to synthesize the different positions and bring them up to the President for decision. I thought that during the Reagan administration, the NSC people who were working on arms control issues did a superb job. There was very good contact between the negotiators in the field and the people in the NSC. We could always count on them to get the bureaucracy to move if we came back and said that a particular issue was blocked and that we needed to change a position, or on other occasions that we needed to hold firm a little longer. The NSC was the place you knew you would eventually have to go to get the right decisions made—not that they themselves necessarily made them, but that they would ensure that a decision was made.

What was the prevailing philosophy on the relation between national defense and arms cuts? I think there was a consistent philosophy on it, one which I happen to support, which essentially held that arms control is but one element of our national security policy. That is, the fundamental importance of any agreement was whether it did or did not enhance our security, and that consequently the two were very closely related.

I wouldn't look at what we were seeking to achieve in terms of arms cuts as much as in terms of arms control and security. I don't think it is correct to seek reductions just for the sake of reductions. What matters is what you end up with—what type of structure there is at the end and what that structure does for security. If the end result of an agreement enhances security, hopefully at lower levels of armaments, then you have made progress. I don't believe in arms control for its own sake, and I think that was a fundamental philosophy of the Reagan Administration.

How much freedom did the negotiators have? I thought I had a fair amount of freedom. I never took any "walk in the woods" in the sense that I went off without any instructions or sense of what the key people in Washington might accept. However, there were a couple of occasions, and one in particular, where I thought we had to move our policy. Reykjavík, you will recall, left each side with 100 warheads outside of Europe. For a number of reasons this, in my view, was not the optimal attainable outcome. I believed we could persuade the Soviets to join us in moving to global zero. The way to achieve this was by making a certain low-cost concession in return for getting back a high-value result.

I handled this by back channels. The use of the back channel is not the prescribed way to proceed, but my proposal was disseminated to the key players in the key agencies in Washington. Only a few people were aware of it. I got a response, and that is how we arrived at global zero. It took careful and sensitive discussions with the Soviets, but I was able to work out the main approach with Washington in advance. However, I was in effect credibly disownable. If for some reason it didn't work out and we determined that the Soviets were merely leading us on, I would be disowned. I realized that and was prepared to accept the consequences if the effort had backfired.

Thus, I have no sense that my freedom was overly circumscribed even on a major issue such as changing an outcome reached at a summit. Moreover, as I pointed out earlier, there were many times when you simply had to make the decisions right there on the spot.

NARRATOR: How were your relations with Paul Nitze? Did he provide a link between you and the secretary and the President?

MR. GLITMAN: As you can tell from my bio, I spent a good deal of time with Paul Nitze. Paul was head of the delegation and I was the deputy for the first two years of the negotiation. He and I tend to approach problems in very much the same way. I find him a very rigorous person in terms of his thinking.

He is capable of saying, "I've changed my mind." In discussion within a delegation, he might start out with one position, but if after hearing the discussion he concludes that the position he started out with is not the best one, he will change it. I admire that in a man, especially one who has had as much experience as he has. We had a very good working relationship.

As he has pointed out in his book, when he went back to Washington after the Soviets walked out on the negotiations, he began to concentrate more on the START (Strategic Arms

Reduction Talks) and SDI (Strategic Defense Initiative) issues and less on INF. He commented that he knew INF was going to be taken care of. We got good support from him, and there was frequent discussion with him.

NARRATOR: *The Economist* in an editorial early in the Kennedy administration said that "either the president drives arms negotiation, or arms negotiation will not progress." Is that a correct estimate of the role of the president? How did President Reagan perform in terms of your INF negotiation? What role did he play?

MR. GLITMAN: There wouldn't be an INF Treaty if it weren't for President Reagan. I took great comfort in knowing two things. First, if I went back to the President and said that we could not get a good treaty—that I didn't think we could get a good deal, to put it in crude terms—or that the American interest would not be served by what I saw coming out of this negotiation, the President would have backed that up. Knowing as a negotiator that the President would back you up if you just folded your books and walked out the door because it wasn't good for the United States gives you a tremendous sense of stability and confidence.

Second, the President clearly saw where he wanted to come out. He never veered from that. He was prepared to be flexible. For example, in the last half of 1982, I began to argue that we couldn't stay exclusively on the zero track forever; that in order to remain credible we would have to offer something that while in keeping with our and our Allies' security needs would be more than zero but less than we were planning to deploy. He was flexible enough to agree to try that, but he never veered from his preference for zero.

There again, it gave one a sense of confidence both in dealing with the Soviets and in the context of interagency discussions, to have a President who clearly said what he preferred but also what he was prepared to accept short of his preference. We knew that if we couldn't get the "best" agreement, as long as the President could be shown that the outcome we did achieve was in keeping with what he wanted to accomplish, he would back it. I think that was a very crucial part of the negotiating process both in Geneva and Washington.

QUESTION: A lot of the commentary on INF while it was going on or late in the Reagan administration dealt with the zero option in a way that sounds very different from your description of Reagan's thinking on that subject. Strobe Talbott and other people saw it as a way of placating public opinion, not as a serious proposal. How did the zero option develop within the administration, and how did it look to the principal negotiators and political decisionmakers?

MR. GLITMAN: First, I think the President believed in the zero option; he did not see it as a ploy to placate public opinion. I am not as sure about everyone in the administration, but I am confident that he saw it sincerely as the outcome he wanted.

How did it start? When we were building up to what eventually became the 1979 decision in NATO, the so-called two-track decision, the discussion of deployments preceded the discussion of arms control. The Soviet deployment of the SS-20 had created a tremendous amount of attention and raised deep concern among our European allies. We had developed ground-launched cruise missiles, and some of the Europeans at that point very much wanted us to keep open the option to deploy them. The reaction to the SALT (Strategic Arms Limitation Talks) II Treaty among some of the Europeans had been very negative, because they feared that we would lose the option to deploy cruise missiles. For some of them the cruise missile had become what I refer to as a King Lear weapon: "I shall do such things; I know not what they may be, but they shall be the terror of the earth." People weren't quite sure what the cruise missile was capable of, but there was a strong sense on the part of many Europeans that we ought not to give up that option. That combination of events led up to the 1979 decision.

The intellectual argument at the time was that there was a gap in the deterrent spectrum which had to be filled in order to ensure that deterrence would continue to work. We had deployed INF missiles in Europe in the 1960s. They were withdrawn at the end of that decade largely because they were obsolete in the case of the

Mace and Matador. In the case of the Jupiter, there is a dispute. Some people say it was in return for the Soviets pulling their missiles out of Cuba. Nitze says no, that they had become obsolete and we were worried about their security. They were, he argues, scheduled to come out.

We had thus gone for several years without any INF missiles in Europe. Nevertheless, there was a feeling, admittedly theoretical, that without the deployment of the ground-launched missiles in Europe the deterrent spectrum would be broken. The Soviets could then mistakenly conclude that they could threaten our Allies and that the United States would not be able to respond. That was very much the heart of the intellectual argument for deployment.

INF differs from START in that the former was much more politically oriented than the latter. At the heart of the INF issue was what I call "the great game of the Cold War period." Indeed, there are some similarities between the "great game" and the one Kipling wrote about between the British and Russians in the Indian subcontinent. At issue was the political orientation of Western Europe: whether it would continue to be allied with the United States, or whether the Soviets could somehow break the Alliance between the United States and Europe with special emphasis on Germany. That is what INF was all about, and that is why it transcended arms control. Consequently, the initial effort was to talk about deployment, the need to fill this gap in the deterrence spectrum: to reassure the Europeans that the alliance remained sound. There also developed a good deal of concern, however, among some of the Europeans that deployment alone was insufficient and that we had to offer a negotiating track.

The origins of the concept of a negotiating track go back to the so-called neutron bomb affair. In that case we were considering what was seen as a rather routine deployment. The proposal was to replace dirtier weapons with cleaner ones which would have less collateral damage and thus be a more credible deterrent. But the press picked it up and labeled it the neutron bomb. Reduced-blast weapon would have been a more accurate name, but obviously not as eye-catching. Over five consecutive days the *Washington Post* hammered away at the "killer bomb." It succeeded in focusing public attention in this country and eventually in Europe on that system. As you will recall, in the end we didn't deploy it, but we said something to the effect that if the Soviets did not deploy the SS-20s, we would not deploy the reduced-blast weapon. Thus, the concept of negotiating on rather than deploying a nuclear weapon system was introduced. Moreover, as you also recall, the Soviets concluded after that affair that they could break the West's will when it came to deployments of nuclear weapons in Europe.

All of that is the background for the topic at hand; i.e., how did we arrive at zero? When we were discussing with the Europeans what should be the end result of an INF negotiation, the question of what should be our preferred number naturally arose. We were going to deploy 572. We couldn't say that this was our bottom line negotiating number; it had to be something below that. The phrase we used was "the lowest feasible number."

The Germans—and I can say this openly because they have taken credit for it—began after awhile to argue that the lowest possible number is zero. They urged that we put zero forward as a "feasible" number but not the only or necessarily the most desirable one. Many others, however, said, "Wait a minute! If our intellectual argument for deployment is based on the premise that we have to fill a gap in the deterrent spectrum, how can we justify proposing zero?" Note that our argument was not based on the existence of the SS-20, because we believed U.S. INF deployments in Europe were required for broader reasons of deterrence.

In any case, the German argument won the day. NATO's position was that we would go to the lowest possible number, which could include zero. The origins of the zero option are therefore German, not American, and you can find articles in which German leaders take credit for this.

Thus, as far back as December 1979 under the Carter administration, the United States said that it could accept a zero solution. What changed under the Reagan administration is that the zero outcome evolved from one of many we could accept to the optimal good. On the way to the position, however, a lot of interagency battles were fought over whether or not zero was a reasonable number to put forward.

In any event, the President thought it was, and throughout the negotiations, we never deviated from saying that this was our preferred outcome. We did—and as I noted earlier, I personally had something to do with that—eventually offer another number, and then another number after that, because it wasn't clear that the Soviets would accept zero. Some of us argued that if we ended up with some deployments, fewer than we had planned on and certainly facing fewer SS-20s and other Soviet INF missiles, we could still have an agreement that improved our national security and that of our Allies.

We ended up with zero, but as I noted it almost ended up with 100 warheads in Soviet Asia and 100 warheads in the United States. But an outcome along those lines, as I said earlier, would not have enhanced our security or that of our Allies, especially Japan.

QUESTION: Did Reagan understand the issue as primarily one of European-American relations rather than of deterrence and the other kinds of arguments that were circulating?

MR. GLITMAN: I'm not sure that I can answer that with any particular insight. Certainly, he argued the point of needing to bring the Allies along; the importance of this for U.S.-Allied relations were not lost on him. He sent George Bush to Europe in 1983 at a very crucial moment, for example, to help rally the Europeans behind deployment.

But my sense is that the disarmament aspect motivated him more than the U.S.-European political-military aspect. The feeling that we could eliminate an entire category of nuclear weapons and enhance our security at the same time was probably more of a driving force.

NARRATOR: One of our guests said that Richard Perle was the first architect of the zero option and that he put it forward because he thought the Soviets would not accept it. Is that apocryphal?

MR. GLITMAN: You would have to ask him, but in any case, that belief is documented in some of the books. Richard Perle was a major exponent of the zero option. He may have been the American godfather, but the grandfather was speaking *auf deutsche*.

QUESTION: How was the relationship between your team and the Defense Department, particularly with the various services whose weapon systems you were challenging? Also, in negotiating, did you have in mind whether what you were doing would sail with the Senate?

MR. GLITMAN: There is a misconception abroad that the military are impossible on arms control issues. My experience was quite the contrary; I found them very sensible. We were fortunate to have General William Burns, who later became ACDA director, as the JCS representative on the INF negotiating team from the beginning and almost until the very end, when he moved first to State and then to ACDA. He was a pleasure to work with at ACDA as well as on the delegation.

The U.S. military kept me, and Paul Nitze before me, fully informed on their requirements and bottom lines for individual weapons systems. We received great support. When we were considering numbers other than zero and needed to know the minimum number of Pershing missiles that we could militarily put in the field, the military representatives did a fine job of not only informing us but also of explaining the rationale. Thus, we knew how low we could go and still have a militarily viable force.

That knowledge gives you a great sense of confidence. That is not the number you are going to throw out at the beginning necessarily, but you know you can fall back to it. I therefore have very positive feelings about cooperation with the uniformed side of the Defense Department.

The civilian side could be a little more difficult. Sometimes one wondered whether some of them wanted a negotiated outcome. Some of them were sincerely convinced that we couldn't get sufficient verification—a major concern on their part. They pushed that agenda to its limits and sometimes beyond what we in the end could accept for ourselves, but we loyally carried out our instructions and we achieved our purposes. We got almost everything we asked for. Moreover, I'm not sure the United States could have lived with what we didn't get.

Next, concerning our relations with the Congress. When we began the process of negotiation, the Senate and the House requested permission to get into the negotiations proper. Quite properly, I think, we said no. I have had personal experience in trade negotiations for which the Constitution does give the Congress more input than it does in other aspects of international relations. Those experiences convinced me that a joint administrative-legislative negotiating team facing representatives from a foreign administration is not a good thing.

In one such instance, we were negotiating, I believe, with the Brazilians. The Congress had insisted that we have members of the relevant congressional committee staffs present in the room, so we had the U.S. administration people on one side of the table with congressional staffers on their flanks and the Brazilians on the other. At one point the Brazilians asked, "If we accept what you are proposing, how do you think the Congress would react?" One of the staffers piped up and said, "No trouble at all!" Then another one said, "Oh yes, there will be!" Naturally, the meeting degenerated at that point. I realized then why the administration negotiating must do the negotiating alone: There are 535 members of Congress and about 18,000 members of the congressional staffs, and no single one of them can speak at the negotiating table for the rest. They speak when they vote, but they can't carry on a negotiation and commit via that process for the rest of that institution. That is one reason why I was not keen on having them actually participate in the negotiation as negotiators.

However, the Congress did set up an observer group for the INF negotiations. At first I thought this might prove to be a problem. I was, in fact, very skeptical, but I was wrong. It turned out to be a great idea.

Senator Ted Stevens (R-Alaska) took the lead on the Senate side. Senator Richard Lugar (R-Indiana), Senator Claiborne Pell (D-Rhode Island), Senator Sam Nunn (D-Georgia), Senator John Warner (R-Virginia), Senator Al Gore (D-Tennessee) were frequent visitors. Many others also came (I hope I'm not leaving anybody out). Fewer people came from the House side, but understandably. They usually came on weekends and on holidays. Finally at one point after we had been going without a day off for some time, I said, "This is the only chance we have to get out of this building. We welcome your presence, but why do you come on weekends and holidays?" One of them quite apologetically said, "We can't help it; it is the only time we can get away!" I realized that they had no choice.

Obviously, there are moments when you are involved in a delicate stage of negotiation and you have to brief them on what is going on. Sometimes someone would say, "I don't agree with what you are doing." On those occasions, I would have to say, "Please, if you don't agree with us, don't tell them that." And they didn't; they were loyal and good about it.

There were times when the members of Congress sensed that we were having difficulty making a point which the legislators supported and that we needed to persuade the Soviets that the position we were taking would be strongly backed up by the Congress. At those times the Senators or Representatives would use the usual cocktail or dinner party and get together with the Soviets (without being intellectually dishonest) to reinforce our argument.

In addition to their visits to us in Geneva, Paul Nitze would meet with them in Washington once a week and brief the Senate and House observers on developments in the negotiations. That, too, was helpful.

They were very helpful and followed the negotiation closely. When the time came for ratification, we had good support from them because they had worked through the problems with us. All in all, our experience with the Congress was very positive.

QUESTION: How did the Soviets view our problems with presenting a single negotiating position on behalf of a divided government? Wouldn't the Soviets have had similar problems of internal governance?

MR. GLITMAN: They probably are having them now, but they didn't have them then. The negotiations began with Brezhnev as Soviet leader and went through the sequence of Andropov, Chernenko, and finally arriving at Gorbachev. But the people across the table from us represented institutions: The Foreign Ministry under Gromyko for most of the time, with Shevardnadze at the end—a happy change; the Defense Ministry; and the KGB.

They did not have the same problems of having to adjust to new administrations as we did, although they had a taste of this at the very end.

At the end, one could sense a little bit of distance between what Gorbachev was saying and what the negotiators were saying. Gaps began to appear between the time we would get assurances from Gorbachev publicly about making certain moves and when the negotiators on the other side of the table would actually present them. We would, of course, call this time lag to their attention, since the Gorbachev position was usually more positive than the negotiators. As time went by, particularly with Shevardnadze there, the time lag became shorter, until it disappeared.

QUESTION: Those institutions, then, really ran the show on their side?

MR. GLITMAN: Yes, and of course the Communist party was the establishment that ran it all. We now know, because they have revealed to the public, how they organized themselves. It was not unlike the way we organized ourselves, but I do recall reading Shevardnadze's complaint at one point that the military did tend to run most of the interagency discussions in Moscow, and that he felt the civilians and the Foreign Ministry should take a larger role.

In general, we had better continuity in our negotiating team than they did, probably for the first time in history. Certainly the core of our group stayed: John Woodworth, who was deputy negotiator when I became negotiator, was the Defense Department representative at the beginning, and General Burns stayed with us almost throughout the whole negotiation. Folks from ACDA were basically the same people, even though they tended to rotate. Even most of the advisers stayed with us. By contrast, on the Soviet side there were changes. They had different chief negotiators, and the rest of their members changed as well. This gave us a clear advantage.

Team continuity is useful in that it allows you to call the other side to account for things they have said in past negotiating sessions. But what really matters is the team spirit and the ability to work as a team. For example, I considered it was helpful that if a member of the delegation had an idea, even if we were at the table negotiating, he or she put it in a note and sent it to me. That annoyed the daylights out of the Soviets! They didn't like that one bit and finally made some sort of comment along the lines of, "Why are you always getting those notes?"

I said, "Well, I don't have all the brains in the world. There are very smart people on this side of the table, and they have good ideas. I want those ideas." I didn't always take the suggestions, but if somebody came up and said, "Remember to ask them this," and I had forgotten, I would ask the Soviets. Or if someone had a good idea or argument that I hadn't thought of, I would throw it out on the table. Oddly enough, this "collective approach" was not visible on the other side. They were far more structured at the table. I take our approach as a reflection of a very strong team spirit.

QUESTION: In the structure of the whole effort, as a generality, wouldn't it be reasonable and efficient to center the policy work entirely in the NSC?

MR. GLITMAN: That can't really be done unless the NSC is expanded enormously, at which point its effectiveness would begin to suffer. Let me put it another way: Each one of the agencies has a particular part of policy for which it has primary responsibility. It is their job to be expert in that area, and it is natural that they will put that part of the policy forward. For example, the State Department will put forward those elements of our foreign policy that are involved in a negotiation.

I mentioned the political side of INF. The State Department would be keeping an eye on that, recognizing that what is at stake is not only the number of weapons we end up with but also what happens to our Alliance. Do the Soviets break NATO or don't they? That would be uppermost in the State Department's mind as it considered a specific development in the negotiations.

The military might be looking at it from the standpoint of the impact of a development in the negotiations on our force structure. The Pentagon's civilian side would be looking at the security issue in perhaps a somewhat broader sense, with ACDA looking at it from the standpoint of the arms control process. All of this has to be brought together, and the NSC would have to duplicate or replicate the entire structure of the government to achieve that same result. The NSC's role changes with administrations, but its traditional role has been to broker the differences between or among the agencies. Increasingly, however, I believe the NSC has also become a player.

I was in the NSC at the end of the Johnson administration and was struck by the fact that there were only, I think, some 17 people on the NSC staff at that time—a very small number. I was doing largely economic work, but we also covered European issues. Let's assume there was a dispute between the Treasury and Commerce Departments and the State Department on a trade issue, and they couldn't resolve it among themselves. Our role as we saw it then was not to get involved unless we could clearly see that the President was going to get involved at some point, or if the agencies couldn't reach an agreement and it required the President to come to closure. When that type of situation arose, the NSC would seek to develop a common position, or failing that, to present clear options to the President.

I should add that we would normally put a little chit on top of the memo outlining the dispute and suggesting courses of action. That is, we received memos from various departments, and our job was to summarize the issue and the agency positions for the national security adviser and the President. Sometimes, however, we would add a line saying that from where we sat it looked as if agency x's view was correct, or that none of the above made any sense and we should consider another approach.

Later I went back to that same office. A friend of mine had taken the job that I had, but it was a new administration. Dr. Kissinger was in charge of the NSC staff. I was waiting to see my friend, and I asked a secretary how things were going. She answered, "Oh, Mr. Glitman, it's terrible here! We're working Saturdays and Sundays; I'm typing my fingers to the bone!" I said, "What do you mean? We didn't prepare long memos." "Oh no," she said, "it has all changed. We are writing enormous papers!"

Indeed it had changed. Under Dr. Kissinger, the NSC, instead of taking what had come from the other agencies and summarizing it and maybe adding a line or two about another approach, was

103

starting to replicate some of the work, adding large dollops of its own input. In sum, the NSC was becoming a player rather than an arbitrator or a broker. I am not saying that one way of organizing is right and the other is wrong. It is just that you can do it different ways.

Can you simultaneously be the honest broker and coordinator, yet have a position of your own? That's the point that I have made occasionally to the people there. You can't do both. In a sense, the NSC lowers itself on the bureaucratic chart; it moves down to the layer of the other agencies the minute it begins to take on the role of an agency participant. Once that happens, its effectiveness as a broker is undermined.

I think that the NSC under the Reagan administration experienced a certain frustration. They had to be very careful, when they put forward their own views, to ensure they did not lose their ability to broker. They were sensitive to that, but there was also this pressure to have an NSC view. It is a dilemma.

QUESTION: When you look at the Soviet Union these days, it strikes me that the chances for rather vigorous efforts at force reductions in both strategic weapons and conventional forces are probably better now than they are going to be five years from now. Are we now up to shaking out our own positions enough to go for large force reductions? I have the feeling that with the successful conclusion of START and CFE (Conventional Armed Forces in Europe), Washington has lost a sense of urgency about going further with the arms reduction process.

MR. GLITMAN: I think there is an element of flux in how Washington is looking at this issue now, partly as a result of the flux in the Soviet Union. You can make arguments in favor of sitting on your hands now: We have just finished the START Treaty; we have finished CFE I; we have a bilateral chemical weapons agreement with the Soviets. All of this has to be absorbed. The START Treaty covers 15 years and will result in a one-third cut with particularly deeper reductions in the most threatening type of weapons, so why not just sit back and absorb these accomplishments? Furthermore, tensions are not as severe as they used to be. The Soviets are withdrawing weapons from Eastern Europe, and budget pressures are such that they will probably take some further cuts. In fact, if you read the Soviet press, you find the post-coup generals are now saying, "We've got to consolidate and downsize!" Thus, there are arguments for taking a break from arms control and one hears them nowadays.

My own view, however, is closer to what you said at the beginning: We do have an opportunity now, but not without risks. It is not clear to whom we are talking, what they represent, or what they will represent in the future. On the other hand, if you carry that to its logical conclusion, we stop talking to them everywhere. I mean, there is somebody sitting in the Soviet seat in the U.N. Security Council right now, so you can overdo the argument that there is no one there to talk to.

Second, I think I am correct in saying that international law normally binds the chosen successor government or entities to what the predecessor had done. If you do start negotiating, you tend to focus the other side on putting somebody forward who can speak for them, and it is up to them to work out how they get their instructions to the field.

Another point that I think needs to be made is that with INF, CFE, and START, we have established precedents for very intrusive verification. If you look at what took up the greatest amount of time in negotiations, especially at the end, it was the verification issues, because they became very technical and because they were what was left at the end. (That is human nature at work: focusing on what's left—because it is all that is left—and making it as important as something that was far more important earlier.)

In any event, my sense is that it need not necessarily take as long the next time around. We do have an opportunity to carry out the June 1990 joint statement that we made with the Soviets in connection with START II. That is, in my view, an excellent starting point. The statement is very broad and is not a Vladivostok-style, semi-detailed agreement or anything of that sort. However, in terms of laying out a road map of where we want to go on the strategic side, it does point in the direction of moving away from unstable systems—that is to say, land-based, fixed, heavy MIRVed (multiple independently targetable re-entry vehicle) missiles—and towards mobile, single-warhead missiles, with more reliance on aircraft and naval systems. All of those are steps in the right direction. In fact, START I does tend to push in that direction already.

My own sense, then, is that we do have an opportunity now to follow up on what was agreed to last year. I think we will probably have to wait for the ratification of START I before we can fully get into the next negotiation, but I believe we do have a real opportunity here to strengthen our security with further strategic arms control treaties.

Things could, of course, deteriorate more in the Soviet Union. It might be difficult at some juncture to know who is able to commit the state or states. But today, at least, there is a body that exists under a transitional arrangement. It is the Presidents of the Republics plus Gorbachev who are now constitutionally in charge, so there is someone to talk to.

I would also note that great concern has been expressed around the world about who is in control of the Soviet weapons and where they are. One way to try to reduce that concern is to get the numbers down. This concern is one more reason we should move ahead on arms control.

Another point to bear in mind is that if you look at the leaders of the republics, every one of them, with the exception of the Georgian leader, are all former members of the Communist party. They all have a habit of working together, and they know each other very well. Nationalism is coming to the fore and could sweep these ties away, but there is a framework there for those people today that would permit some measure of cooperation among them in dealing with nuclear arms control negotiations.

I am not saying this "old comrade network" is a good thing; it is a fact. It provides one more reason for us to try to move ahead and reduce the number of weapons. In making this statement, I should emphasize again that I don't believe numbers are the be all and end-all of arms control. It is the quality of the force that is left, and ultimately the security of the United States that should be at the heart of the endeavor.

NARRATOR: That is a good summary point on which to end. A number of people have said to me, "If you want to know what happened at Geneva and Vienna, you should have Ambassador Glitman speak at the Miller Center." I think if anything, they understated this opportunity. We are grateful to you for sharing your knowledge with us.

CHAPTER SIX

Arms Control: Myths, Presidents, Transitions, and Costs*

AMBASSADOR RALPH EARLE

NARRATOR: Ambassador Ralph Earle is former director of the Arms Control and Disarmament Agency (ACDA). In this capacity he served as adviser for arms control and disarmament to the president, the NSC, and the State Department. From 1978 to 1980 he was chief U.S. negotiator, with the rank of ambassador, for the SALT II Treaty. Earlier still, he was ACDA's representative on the U.S. SALT delegation. He has been an officer in the U.S. Army Corps of Engineers and Counterintelligence Corps. Ambassador Earle is a graduate of Harvard College and Harvard Law School.

MR. EARLE: One of the most important tasks in the field of arms control is to destroy, or at least alter, some of the mythology that has emerged over the years concerning arms control. Somebody writes something, it gets repeated, and after 10 or 15 years, what may have been inaccurate in the beginning becomes an article of faith. One of these myths is reflected in a Miller Center publication, which says:

Presented in a Forum at the Miller Center of Public Affairs on 11 May 1992.

Early in the Carter administration arms talks with the Soviet Union broke down, in part because of Soviet objections to the administration's human rights campaign. Negotiations on SALT II were long delayed. Carter gave full attention to the Panama Canal Treaty, and by the time negotiations were resumed, the President's influence in the Senate had waned, and the Soviet invasion of Afghanistan had occurred.

In fact, this is an ongoing myth. I pulled out my diary for 1977, looking particularly at the point where the early talks broke down. President Carter was inaugurated in January 1977. After a review by the new National Security Council, Secretary of State Cyrus Vance met on 28 and 29 March with General Secretary Brezhnev in Moscow. Negotiations were not long delayed; they were renewed less than two months after Carter's inauguration.

The so-called comprehensive proposal that was made at that time was rejected out of hand. I hadn't seen the proposal until we boarded the plane headed for Moscow. When I saw it, I predicted that the Soviets would reject it in four days. I was wrong—they rejected it in three.

They didn't reject it because of the human rights issue. They rejected it because it represented an effort to change a deal that Brezhnev and Ford had made at Vladivostok in 1974. It overreached the Vladivostok deal on which Brezhnev had expended a great deal of political capital with his own people in Moscow. On several occasions Brezhnev left the room in order to make telephone calls. He was clearly calling the military to clear things with them.

In my view, the human rights campaign had very little, if anything, to do with the rejection of that proposal. Another myth was that this comprehensive proposal and its rejection killed the possibility of SALT II ever being successful because so much time was lost after the Soviets made that rejection on 30 March. In reality, it only cost us five or six weeks at most. Again I consulted my calendar, finding that on 13 May, six weeks later, we were in Geneva meeting with the Soviets. On the 18th, 19th, and 20th of May, Secretary Vance came to Geneva and met with Gromyko. We went full blast in our negotiations with several sessions a week until the 19th of August, when we took a week's break; we then continued thereafter.

From the beginning, President Carter had an intense interest in arms negotiations that continued throughout the period. There is no question that some of the things he did undermined the possibility of eventual success of SALT II. One was the political capital he expended on getting the Panama Canal treaties ratified. Republicans like Howard Baker went along with the Panama Canal treaties, but they were unwilling to pay the heavy political price of ratifying another treaty when SALT II came up. The other, far greater blow to the SALT process was the normalization of relations with China in 1978.

By the beginning of December 1978, we had made a great deal of progress with the SALT II treaty, but we by no means had completed it. There were still a number of unresolved issues, some of them major—such as how to deal with the Soviet heavy ICBM launchers and encryption. It bothered me when the White House began to talk optimistically about the treaty being completed within a month or two. I was morally certain that this was impossible, unless one side just rolled over and accepted the proposals of the other, which I knew wouldn't happen. The White House was talking about a summit between Carter and Brezhnev to sign the treaty in February, or even January, in Washington. At that point I was the chief negotiator, and I was getting nervous because I didn't think I was going to be able to produce a treaty for them to sign.

At the same time, however, the process of normalizing relations with the People's Republic of China was progressing. In one of the more unfortunate press conferences, the national security adviser, Dr. Brzezinski, was asked how the normalization process tied in with the proposed visit of General Secretary Brezhnev. In effect, Brzezinski's reply was, "Don't worry about that. Deng Xiaoping is coming in January and we will fit Brezhnev in either before or after that." You can imagine the reaction on the Soviet side upon hearing that the head of one of the only two superpowers in the world was going to be fitted into an otherwise busy schedule in Washington.

Secretary Vance, a great man in my view, arrived in Geneva on about 20 December for a series of meetings with Foreign Minister Gromyko. Mr. Vance was quite tired from a series of commutes to and from the Middle East. The first day went pretty well. They were trying to resolve the difficult issues and move the negotiations forward. On the second morning, however, Gromyko made a long statement about the dangers to world security caused by remotely piloted vehicles (RPVs), known in the vernacular as "drones." These RPVs are aircraft used as targets or occasionally for reconnaissance. None of them are long-range. We were all stunned by Gromyko's remarks, and we took a break. It was one of the few times I have ever seen Secretary Vance angry. He asked, in effect, "What is going on here? You didn't tell me about the RPVs." I replied, "Because I didn't know about it. I have never heard that phrase used in Geneva in six years."

The issue of RPVs was clearly a red herring. We immediately cabled Washington: How many do we have? How many do they have? Where are they? Do they threaten the security of the world? The people in the Pentagon were running around in circles because nobody knew—or had previously cared—how many RPVs we or the Soviets had. This red herring remained on the table when Secretary Vance boarded the plane for home on 23 December 1978. After Vance left, the Soviet negotiators didn't force the issue at all. We finally disposed of it in the treaty with an innocuous reference to RPVs, discounting their danger.

Clearly, the Soviets were telling us that they intended to approach the SALT Treaty on their own terms; they were not going to let us tell them when we were going to complete the treaty. One can argue that this hurt SALT because nothing was accomplished between Vance and Gromyko in the remaining 36 hours in Geneva. The treaty might otherwise have been completed in March. Maybe not; one never knows. As it was, we didn't complete it until June 1979, so we lost anywhere from one to three months as a result of the normalization of relations with China.

This delay in turn pushed the Senate ratification hearings into the summer of 1979, when the Soviet brigade that had already been in Cuba for 25 years was "discovered." I call the Soviet brigade the "banana peel" of the SALT II process. The treaty was not out of the Senate Foreign Relations Committee until 9 November, so the full Senate could not consider the treaty until January. Meanwhile, the Soviets invaded Afghanistan in December, and President Carter asked Senate Majority Leader Robert Byrd to delay Senate consideration. Things went from bad to worse. The idea that the delay at the beginning was crucial, I think, is a myth. The delay toward the end was probably more crucial.

It's funny, but nations really have personalities. Their feelings get hurt and they get angry. Certainly the Soviets had hurt feelings and were angry when this happened.

I would like to quickly summarize the attitude toward arms control of the three presidents for whom I worked. I worked most closely with President Carter and his administration. He was intensely interested in arms control issues. Occasionally, I would be in Washington, away from Geneva, for a meeting of the SCC, a Cabinet-level group chaired by Brzezinski and Vance that met almost biweekly to discuss SALT issues. It was attended by Harold Brown, Stansfield Turner, and others. The President would frequently drop in, and the meeting would become a meeting of the National Security Council.

It was clear that President Carter was familiar with my cables. In fact, he once said to me, "I read every one of your cables." I was aghast, because I didn't read all my cables. He couldn't possibly have read them all, but I think he did read all the summaries and all the substance, because he was always well informed in those meetings. Carter has been criticized for being too involved in detail, but whether or not his involvement was excessive, he certainly knew the details of the SALT Treaty.

Another important thing about the Carter administration was that Secretary Vance frequently conducted what we referred to as "back channel" meetings with Dobrynin in Washington and occasionally communicated with Gromyko when they were both in New York at the United Nations. Gromyko sometimes came to Washington to meet with President Carter as well.

Secretary Vance and his special assistant for Soviet affairs, Marshall Shulman, kept those of us in Geneva fully informed of those conversations, which was a tremendous improvement over the Nixon-Kissinger team's pattern of telling us absolutely nothing about those meetings. In fact, when President Ford went to Vladivostok to meet with Brezhnev, it was the first time in the history of individual summits—with just the President and the foreign ministers present—that there had been an American official present who understood Russian. In other words, Nixon and Kissinger had been dealing with Brezhnev all those years through a Soviet interpreter, and the only person taking notes was Kissinger. One of the benefits of having an interpreter is that the good ones are also basically stenographers—they write down everything that both parties say because then they have to read it back. An interpreter doesn't interrupt the President of the United States saying, "Wait a minute, you are going too fast." Since the president may talk for 10 or 15 minutes without stop, the interpreter must rely on his notes.

In the Nixon era, we didn't have such notes. I am told that once Henry Kissinger had a gap in his notes and called the Soviet interpreter to ask him to fill them in, which the interpreter refused to do. With Kissinger being the only one taking notes, records of meetings were not widely distributed. Those of us in Geneva learned nothing. The really frustrating thing was that Gromyko kept Minister Vladimir Semyonov in Geneva apprised of what happened in the Kissinger meetings, so Semyonov had the advantage in terms of what was going on in the background.

When Kissinger and Gromyko would met in Geneva, they would alternate venues—once the Soviet place, once the American place. The Soviet choice was always the Soviet mission; the American choice was the Intercontinental Hotel. As a result, none of us on the delegation were ever present at any of those meetings. When Malcolm Toon became U.S. ambassador to Moscow, he asked me how much we in Geneva knew about the back channel. I said, "Well, Mac, when Gromyko is in Geneva, after the meetings Kissinger sends one of his staff down to brief Alex Johnson [then the head of our delegation], and I think he tells him about 60 percent of what happened. Then Alex briefs the delegation, and he tells us about 60 percent of what he has learned. So, we get about 36 percent of the discussion." It was very frustrating.

The secrecy was intense in the Nixon administration. It was better in the Ford administration, but Kissinger was still running the show then. In the Carter administration, Mr. Vance or usually

Marshall Shulman or Paul Warnke would call me in Geneva and tell me what had happened. If there were some papers exchanged, we might be sent copies. So, communication was much better during the Carter administration.

The transition of arms control teams from one presidency to the next is important. I am not a career government person, but I have been through five transitions, and I have never seen a really good one. It is sort of like saying I don't live in California but I have been through five earthquakes. With the exception of the Nixon to Ford transition, I thought all the transitions were awful. When Nixon succeeded Johnson, the Johnson administration had been ready to announce the beginning of SALT negotiations in August 1968. Then the Soviets invaded Czechoslovakia, and it was deferred. The Nixon administration changed all the personnel, restudied the program, and then came up with exactly the program that Johnson had used, after wasting eight months.

Perhaps the worst transition—and few people realize it—was the Nixon to Nixon transition following his reelection in 1972. It certainly was a disaster in the arms control area. Gerry Smith left of his own accord as the chief negotiator and head of the Arms Control and Disarmament Agency, but almost everyone else was purged. Royal Allison, a brilliant, dedicated, and effective three-star Air Force general was ousted after Senator Henry Jackson complained to Nixon that Allison had not been hard-nosed enough. Ray Garthoff was made an inspector in the State Department. Paul Nitze stayed, but he was the only one. The whole affair was deeply embarrassing.

The Nixon to Ford transition was not traumatic in any way because Kissinger remained the secretary of state and the national security apparatus functioned pretty much as it had before.

The Ford to Carter transition was difficult. I think the problem is that every group feels that since they got their man elected president, they can do anything better than the incumbent. When the Carter transition team came in, they talked to one member of the delegation, Alex Johnson, for one hour—entirely about housing in Geneva! That was the extent of their interest. I had been a member of the delegation for five years at that time, yet nobody talked to me about the delegation's work.

The Carter to Reagan shift was another horror. I resigned as head of the Arms Control and Disarmament Agency, as did my deputy, Spurgeon Keeny. The four assistant directors—two of whom had been appointed by Carter, one by Ford, and one by Nixon—all had their resignations accepted within ten days. Three of those positions remained unfilled for over a year. The Reagan people thought they were getting rid of the rascals, but they had no real view as to where negotiations were going.

The final blow during the Reagan transition, in my view, came when Lieutenant General Ed Rowny, who had been the representative of the Joint Chiefs of Staff on the Carter delegation, was made the chief negotiator. General Rowny had done—and I think Ed would confirm this if he were here—everything he could to prevent us from getting a treaty. Making him chief negotiator was quite a signal to the Soviets.

Transitions are not necessarily the key to continued success in arms control, but they give some indication of the importance the new administration accords arms control, as well as some indication of the intelligence and seriousness with which they will approach arms control issues.

QUESTION: How are people on the outside to interpret the inner workings of the negotiating process when an event occurs such as occurred immediately after the Soviet rejection? National Security Adviser Brzezinski went on television the morning after the Soviet rejection with a lengthy explanation of what had happened. As part of that briefing, he made the statement, admittedly following intense questioning about human rights, that if the U.S. government and the Carter administration in particular ever had to choose between its human rights campaign and a SALT II Treaty, it would choose the human rights campaign. The strong suggestion was that the Carter administration had made just this calculation, placing the treaty secondary to human rights.

MR. EARLE: I didn't mean to suggest that human rights was not a factor, but I do think the treaty would have been rejected regardless. It has become increasingly apparent that the national security adviser rated an arms control treaty as a low priority. In fact, I spoke recently with a graduate student who is writing her thesis on the normalization of relations with China and she concludes that the more deeply she explores relations with China, the more she realizes how closely related they were to the SALT Treaty. She has interviewed many people, and it has become clear to her that the national security adviser thought little of arms control and was quite prepared to sacrifice it. Whether he spoke for the President in that press conference, it is hard to tell. I'm sure human rights was a major issue for President Carter, but so was SALT.

QUESTION: How sincere over the years has each side been about making real arms reductions?

MR. EARLE: The first thing we felt we had to do was to level the playing field. I think strategic stability already existed, but we had to make sure that it was on a firm foundation. I get upset when people say the START Treaty is the first treaty that has provided for a reduction in weapons. If SALT II had been ratified, the Soviets would have had to eliminate about 10 percent of their weapons systems.

Were we sincere about reductions? The goal of arms reductions was certainly on everyone's mind, especially in the Carter administration, which was probably the most arms-control oriented. The concept of stability drove the positions that were taken: The feeling was that if we could get this treaty calling for equal aggregates of central system, ICBMs, SLBMs, and heavy bombers, we could go to reductions. In fact, at the Vienna summit of 1979, President Carter proposed to General Secretary Brezhnev that the SALT II Treaty be amended to make further reductions of 10 percent each year for the five-year life of the treaty. It was clearly in Carter's mind and in all of our minds that this was the beginning, not the end, of discussions on strategic arms.

Brezhnev's capacities were slipping at that time. He was not focusing very well and didn't respond to Carter's suggestion. Then, of course, the things we mentioned earlier happened, so there could not have been a follow-up. At any rate, the treaty was never ratified.

We are finally on the road to reductions. I think we are going too slow, given the new situation in the world. Numbers in and of themselves are not the crucial measure of security. Sometimes you are safer with 10,000 on each side than you are with 1,000. If we each had 100 missiles and they were all MIRVs, it would be a very insecure situation. We would be much better off with 10,000 single warhead missiles, because there would be no temptation to launch; with 100 MIRVs, there is.

The production of nuclear weapons is very wasteful. I was happy to see in the newspaper this morning that for the first time in 45 years, the United States is not producing any new nuclear weapons. At least that is a step in the right direction. I think American nuclear stockpiles will be reduced to roughly 6,000 accountable warheads if and when START is ratified—which I think it will be—but we can go much lower than that. We are going in the right direction mostly because of recent events in what used to be the Soviet Union.

QUESTION: Taking into account the dissolution of the Soviet Union, with whom shall we negotiate?

MR. EARLE: This is the key current issue in arms control. There are four former Soviet republics that have nuclear weapons on their soil: Russia, Belarus, Ukraine, and Kazakhstan. Belarus doesn't seem to be a problem; after Chernobyl, they want to get rid of their nuclear weapons as fast as they can. It is believed that all of the tactical nuclear weapons have now been removed from the other three republics to Russia for dismantling and elimination.

The problem arises with the strategic weapons, of which there are over 1,500 in both Ukraine and Kazakhstan. In fact, if they keep them, they will become the third and fourth largest nuclear states in the world, surpassing Britain, France, and China. President Kravchuk of Ukraine was in Washington recently, and we think he has agreed—he changes his position almost weekly—that by 1996 all of the strategic weapons in his country will be gone. The president of Kazakhstan is coming to Washington soon, and the United States hopes to get a comparable commitment from him.

118

If all this occurs, we hope they will join the Non-Proliferation Treaty as nonnuclear weapon states, which is a commitment they have indicated they would give. As a matter of fact, Kravchuk said he would sign any time. He should have been handed a pen on the spot. If this does happen, it will of course be Russia with whom we will be negotiating.

This is a tricky situation. If you were a Ukrainian living next to a common border with Russia, a country with many nuclear weapons and believed to be making plans to take part of your territory, would you give up all your nuclear weapons immediately? Wouldn't you hang on to a few for insurance? The same logic applies to Kazakhstan.

I think it is going to work, and I think it is very important that we and the rest of the world put a great deal of pressure on them—withholding economic assistance, for example—until we have firm commitments and performance of those commitments. I hope we will be negotiating with Russia, but this is not yet certain.

COMMENT: You spoke earlier about the need for Soviet negotiators to obtain approval from the military during the Vladivostok talks. The military is now in such disarray in all of these states that negotiators face a tremendous problem in securing military support for negotiations. They aren't even sure who their enemy is at this point. This utter chaos must make negotiations more difficult.

MR. EARLE: Yes, I would think so. When your counterpart across the table may not have the authority to enforce your agreements, the whole process is weakened.

The organization with which I am involved, the Lawyers' Alliance for World Security, like all nonprofit organizations, has problems raising money. We have a lot of trouble now because the attitude is, "The Berlin Wall has fallen; the Soviet Union has collapsed; the world is safe."

In many respects, however, I think you can argue that the world is much more dangerous right now than it was. There are rumors, which by the best authority are untrue, that some of these

119

tactical nuclear weapons have been sold to Iran and that Gadhafi also has been trying to purchase some.

There are also other problems besides the weapons themselves, the weapons-grade material problem, for example. Obviously, the security over this material is not quite as great as security over the weapons themselves. There is also the problem of the nuclear "brain drain." There are people in the ex-Soviet Union with nuclear know-how who are making pitiful wages now and can be offered a villa on the Mediterranean by Mr. Gadhafi. These are things that we should and must try to do something about, and the sooner the better. The longer this goes on, the greater the possibility of a loss of a weapon, some material, or a scientist.

QUESTION: I have two questions. You said that we should do something about these problems quickly. Why aren't we doing so? My second question is, why don't we have negotiators who are fluent in Russian?

MR. EARLE: I can't provide an answer for your first question. Congressman Les Aspin, chairman of the House Armed Services Committee, said we should set aside a billion dollars to deal with Soviet nuclear weapons. He ended up with $400 million.

Four years ago if somebody had asked the President and Congress what it would be worth to have the Soviet Union collapse in the fashion that it has collapsed, trillions of dollars would have been offered to acquire that result. I guess the simple answer is that it is an election year. Sending money to the former Soviet Union in a year when we had riots in Los Angeles is not very good politics.

As to why we don't have negotiators who speak Russian, many people simply didn't learn Russian, but I think it is important that we do. More important is an understanding of Russian culture, and learning the Russian language would be part of that. If I were picking an ideal delegation today, I would make certain that all members had this sort of cultural background, because that is the real source of misunderstanding.

Good interpreters help. Our interpreters were always better than their interpreters, because ours were born in Russia while none of their interpreters were born in an English-speaking country. All of their interpreters had learned their English as a second language, whereas with our interpreters, it was their native tongue.

The biggest problem in negotiations—whether it is arms control, strategic arms negotiations, or buying a house—is understanding what motivates your adversary. In the negotiations that we had with the Soviets over the years, there was a tremendous absence of understanding on both sides. We certainly didn't understand their system or know much about it. I studied some Russian history and literature when I was in college, so I know a little bit about Russian culture, but by no means a lot. Many of our delegation had no training in Russian culture.

Their chief negotiator was Deputy Foreign Minister Vladimir Semyonov, who had been one of their senior diplomats. He also had been high commissioner of East Germany. At the beginning of the Carter administration, many congressmen came over to look at the negotiations and meet with the Soviets. I particularly remember a visit that John Glenn made. He was very unhappy with the American position on the encryption of telemetry from tests of ICBMs. In a lunch that he and I had with Semyonov, he expressed his unhappiness with both the American and Soviet positions. Semyonov just couldn't understand that a Democratic senator would criticize the policies and positions of a Democratic president. He said to me afterwards, "What kind of a country have you got?" We said, "A democratic country." More and more of our diplomats do speak Russian.

The problem the State Department is facing today is that it is opening embassies in the countries that have emerged from the former Soviet Union, and we don't have anyone who can speak Tajikistani, for example, or some of the languages of the other republics. There is only one person in the State Department who speaks Uzbeki.

QUESTION: My question is related to presidential transitions and how arms negotiations differ from one administration to another. I would like to preface my question with some quotations from the works of President Carter, Alexander Haig, and President Nixon.

The following paragraph is from President Carter's book *Keeping Faith*:

> SALT I was signed in May 1972, and almost immediately the negotiations commenced on somewhat more definitive agreements on SALT II. When President Ford went to Vladivostok in November 1974 to meet with Leonid Brezhnev, they made some progress in developing the framework for further negotiations, spelling out the maximum number of intercontinental missiles each nation could deploy—2,400—and how many of these long-range missiles could contain more than one warhead—1,320. Of the unresolved issues, the primary one involved a Soviet bomber called the Backfire. The Soviets claimed it had only medium-range capability and was not a strategic weapon. But the Americans suspected it might be modified so that it could strike the United States.

What I would like to stress here from what I read is our suspicion that they may have a long-range bomber rather than one of medium capability.

The following excerpt is from Alexander Haig's book *Caveat*:

> The Soviets have continued to deploy SS-20s at the rate of approximately two a week while the European Arm Reduction Talks have been going on in Geneva and despite the fact that Brezhnev in March 1982 had stated that Moscow would observe a moratorium on the placement of SS-20s while the talks were in progress. By late September 1983, the number of SS-20s targeted in Western Europe had risen to 351, or 1,053 warheads. This meant that 1,100 Soviet medium-range nuclear warheads were aimed at Western Europe, which is from the European point of view a grave new strategic danger.

Finally, let me read from President Nixon's book *Seize the Moment*. President Nixon is referring to START negotiations. The earlier quotations referred to SALT. "The focus of new arms control efforts," Nixon writes,

> should be on reducing the number of ICBMs carrying multiple warheads capable of destroying first-strike targets. President Bush's proposal to eliminate such missiles was on the mark, but Gorbachev rejected it. In the absence of such a comprehensive solution, we must insist on rectifying four flaws in START. . . . First, the permitted number of Soviet heavy ICBMs should be reduced from 154 to 77. . . . When the Reagan administration agreed on the first figure, it assumed that the limits would apply to the SS-18 and Model IV.

The major point made by Carter, Haig, and Nixon concerns the Soviet attitude toward negotiations. It seems to me that they always try to negotiate to their strategic advantage in any way possible.

I have two questions. How can we still make mistakes in assuming that this is what they were going to do, and why were we not more careful in this issue when President Nixon stated that the warheads should have been 77 rather than 154? Finally, with the collapse of the former Soviet Union, will we have the same attitude toward the Russians that we had with the Soviets? I assume we still have the same negotiators.

MR. EARLE: First, in response to your last question, I think the people running Russia now are entirely different from those running the Soviet Union before, so our attitude will be different.

Let me discuss some of the individual issues you have raised. The Soviets were right about the Backfire bomber. It is not an intercontinental bomber; it is a medium-range bomber. Frankly, one of the more embarrassing moments in our negotiating history was after the Vladivostok meeting, where, as President Carter mentions, the Backfire bomber became an issue. On a flight from Vladivostok to Beijing with the American press, Dr. Kissinger acknowledged that the Backfire was not a heavy bomber, which was recorded by the press. That incident didn't prevent him from telling us in Geneva to continue insisting that it was a heavy bomber. This incident was a little embarrassing, since Kissinger's press conference had been transcribed and was available to Soviet correspondents in the State Department press room.

As to the SS-20 increase, they were under no obligation to reduce or limit the number of SS-20s they built during that period. They said they would, but they didn't. That was not a very encouraging thing, but there was no binding obligation.

I don't understand Mr. Nixon saying that having gone from 308 to 154, we ought to go to 77. I think we should go to zero. I don't understand why 77 is the magic number. It is just half of half.

The really important thing is that we are dealing with different people in Russia today. Beginning with Mr. Gorbachev's speech at the United Nations on 7 December 1988 when he said that he would unilaterally withdraw a number of forces from East Germany and Eastern Europe (and in fact he did), the director of Central Intelligence said, "That eliminates the possibility of a surprise attack by Soviet ground forces." Gorbachev did this unilaterally. Brezhnev or Stalin would never would have done that, but Gorbachev did, and I think Yeltsin continues the trend. So we really are dealing with different people.

COMMENT: The point that President Nixon is referring to is that reduction from 154 to 77 would bring the Soviets into compliance with the START agreement.

MR. EARLE: The START agreement is not in force, so there is no such obligation. They have 308 launchers of SS-18 MIRV ICBMs. The START agreement provides that they reduce them by 154. This is a problem, because a large number of those SS-18s lie outside of Russia itself and Russia may not have control over them. Maybe they do; I don't know. The new Commonwealth of Independent States (CIS) has control.

QUESTION: Who now carries the Russian nuclear briefcase? Are those who don't have it nonetheless capable of triggering any action?

MR. EARLE: The "football," as we call it, or the briefcase, as they call it, was formally handed over to Yeltsin, and he now has it. It is clear that the strategic weapons, particularly the ICBMs, cannot be launched by the Kazakhs or the Ukrainians without those launch codes.

Tactical nuclear weapons are a different story. The republics all say the tactical nuclear weapons have been transferred to Russia, but there remains some doubt. A tactical nuclear weapon can be as small as a suitcase or an artillery shell. In fact, many of them *are* artillery shells. They are more easily transported, more easily hidden, and unfortunately, more easily detonated than strategic weapons.

The briefcase that Mr. Yeltsin has cannot actually prevent the use of tactical nuclear weapons. In an American combat division, an artillery battalion commander is physically able to launch an artillery shell armed with a nuclear warhead that will detonate at the appropriate time. There are many checks and balances in command procedure and security over such weapons, but our ICBMs in North Dakota and Montana *cannot* be launched without explicit authorization from the National Command Authority.

Submarines present a different problem. We previously had a two-key system on submarines, but now have a three-key system. This means that three officers have to agree to launch a missile and turn keys to do it. The Soviets, I think, have comparable security on their submarines.

I'm not too worried, although I am a little concerned about the tactical nuclear weapons. Even if they all have been transferred to Russia and are not a direct threat to the United States, they could still cause a great deal of trouble for the surrounding republics or for some of their indigenous ethnic minorities.

QUESTION: You spoke of the importance of cultural understanding for successful diplomacy. This seems to be a basic element of any negotiations–economic, military, or whatever. Why, for so long, have our representatives downplayed these cultural bases as a prerequisite to fruitful negotiations?

MR. EARLE: There has been such an effort in our foreign service among our professional diplomats. Likewise, we educate our military in an extraordinary fashion. When I was the principal deputy in International Security Affairs (ISA), which was sort of the policy body of the Pentagon, we had about 150 active duty officers. All of them had master's degrees, and I would say half had doctorates. (Whether their doctorates were in physics or in Russian culture, I can't say.) We do not have a monolithic government; we can't tell people that they must study Russian. We can instruct our foreign service and military officers in Russian, but many of us who come into the government are not career people. Negotiators, on the whole, tend to be private-sector lawyers.

I'm not suggesting, of course, that our negotiations be handled exclusively by career government people. I don't think we get brilliant people like Cy Vance, Paul Warnke, and Harold Brown through the career system. I think we would be less well off had such people like them not gone into the government and if we had relied solely on the career people.

On the other hand, I think there are far too many political appointees in ambassadorial posts. The appointment process borders on scandal: x dollars gets you Luxembourg, 10 x dollars gets you Belgium, and 100 x dollars gets you France. It isn't done quite like that; it's far more subtle.

Clearly, Americans have become more educated about other cultures. In Wendell Willkie's words, we are increasingly becoming "one world." In this country it is still a slow process because many continue to think that if we speak loud enough, everybody will understand us. In speaking of the importance of understanding other cultures, I'm reminded of something that happened during the SALT I talks when Gerard Smith was the chief negotiator dealing with Semyonov. Referring to a series of closely related issues, Gerry apparently said, "Look, if we can just get the first olive out of the bottle, then the others will follow." He said this on several occasions. The skeptical look on Semyonov's face was explained by the fact that in Russia, olives come in a jar with a large opening.

QUESTION: You spoke of the problem of loose nuclear weapons. Do we have any way of knowing if one got loose in Europe, the

Middle East, or elsewhere? Is there any way of knowing where a nuclear missile was coming from before it hit? Would we know where to retaliate?

MR. EARLE: If it were being delivered by a missile, we could pinpoint its origin. If it were simply a loose nuclear weapon, it couldn't get here; the only ones that can reach the United States would be intercontinental ballistic missiles. We have ICBM sensors everywhere, so we would know its origin the moment it was launched.

The problem with loose nuclear weapons is getting them here. Libya, for example, has no means of delivery other than putting a bomb on a ship and sailing it into New York harbor. I keep reminding people of the limits of the Strategic Defense Initiative—if you can't stop a Piper Cub from delivering a bail of marijuana, you are not going to stop a nuclear warhead going 17,000 miles per hour. Besides, if a nuclear weapon detonates aboard a ship of Liberian registry anchored in New York harbor, we still may not be certain where it came from.

QUESTION: How destructive are these loose nuclear weapons, these suitcase bombs? How powerful could one of these small bombs be?

MR. EARLE: They vary, but I would say the most powerful one would be similar to the Hiroshima bomb.

QUESTION: Are those the only kind of weapon that can reach us other than ones smuggled into the country?

MR. EARLE: Only warheads carried by long-range missiles or long-range bombers, which take seven or eight hours to get here, can reach us. Another possibility is submarine-launched weapons, but again, the submarines are all controlled, we hope, by Mr. Yeltsin. Virtually all of these weapons are far more powerful than those dropped on Hiroshima and Nagasaki.

QUESTION: Do you have any hope that nuclear weapons will ever be eliminated from this earth?

MR. EARLE: I am not very optimistic about it; the genie is out of the bottle. The knowledge is public. A Princeton undergraduate wrote a book ten years ago on how to build a nuclear bomb, and he was accurate.

I was speaking at the United Nations a couple of weeks ago and heard a former Canadian ambassador for disarmament make a pitch for total elimination—complete transparency, open skies, and public information about weapons systems and nuclear budgets. I doubt this will happen in my lifetime; it will probably never happen because of the threat of the hidden bomb. The fear I have is that the good guys—and let's include Russia and China for the moment—would all scrap their weapons, but then Gadhafi would say: "I've got one." This scenario is terrifying to me.

What we really need is increased transparency. The Russians have been reading our *Congressional Record* for years. They know how much money we spend on bomb production and so forth, though we do have "black" budgets, too. Now we will have the opportunity to read *their* official records.

One can make the argument that we are better off with nuclear weapons than without them on the theory that if you got rid of all of them and became complacent, how would you deal with some future Hitlerian figure? What if he had 1,000 tanks, and you only had ten—and no nuclear weapons? Still, it is not an issue that I worry about in the near term.

QUESTION: Somewhere I read that Soviet ICBMs are still being produced and that the existing ones are still targeted. Is that true?

MR. EARLE: I think the production lines are still open. The Russians are not unique in continuing production; one is reminded of our Seawolf submarine production. I'm sure the Russians' weapons are still targeted, although Yeltsin said a couple of months ago that he was no longer going to target cities. We already knew that they had been targeting cities, but it was an interesting admission.

128

We don't target cities, per se. We target military-industrial targets. It just so happens that military industrial targets are located in cities. We target all the railroad stations in Moscow, but we are not targeting Moscow. I think that is a euphemistic way of saying we don't target Moscow. I'm sure they are still targeted.

NARRATOR: Who decides on risk? There was a report recently on all the networks saying that we were, in fact, stopping research—not launching or testing—but research on SDI. I don't know where it came from or whether it is right. It is probably not true, but if it were true, wouldn't it be ironic if we were halting SDI research considering this research was the stumbling block to a more substantial reduction in Reykjavík? President Reagan talked in terms of zero missiles, but even agreement on a reduction of a thousand missiles would have been a triumph. Who decides what offers are to be made during the statesmen's walk in the woods? Who should make these momentous decisions?

MR. EARLE: I think it should be a joint decision of Congress and the executive branch. Chairman Les Aspin has recently done a great deal of useful work in this area. Some of Aspin's work is really very good in determining how much money we need to spend to maintain a solid base of research, knowledge, and development. I think the executive—including the military—should be assessing that all the time.

I am a strong opponent of SDI as an end in itself, but I am a strong proponent of continued research in the area. I would not like to see us just drop the whole idea. We are spending a great deal of money on things that aren't going to work. Before the President's speech in March 1983, we were already spending more than a billion dollars a year on ballistic missile defense research. I thought that was fine, and I think we ought to continue to do that.

The problem we face, which was addressed in the *Washington Post* recently regarding submarine production, is how to maintain the skills of people in the military industry without continued production. Les Aspin thinks we can, for a modest amount, keep expertise alive without spending massive amounts of money on acquisition of weapons systems. I'm no expert on it, but Les has done a great deal of study and has had a lot of good people working on it, as has the Pentagon and others.

I don't know the answer. I don't know how you keep welders skilled in Groton, Connecticut, without building Seawolf submarines, but apparently there is a way to do it. I think we should do it because in the long run it would not be that expensive compared to what we are presently spending now in acquisition of systems.

NARRATOR: Each time Ralph Earle is here we gain a stronger overview of arms control. He is our teacher in this field, and we are grateful that he has conducted yet another fruitful class.

CHAPTER SEVEN

President Warren G. Harding and the Congress: Arms Control and the Washington Conference Treaties*

THOMAS BUCKLEY

NARRATOR: Thomas Buckley is the author of the classic work on the Washington Conference, *The United States and the Washington Conference, 1921-1922,* which received the award as the best first book by a historian. He is a co-author of *American Foreign and National Security Policies, 1914-1945,* editor of *Research and Roster Guide of the Society of Historians of American Foreign Relations,* and has written many articles and contributed many chapters to books. He is a graduate of Indiana University, which has an outstanding program in diplomatic history.

MR. BUCKLEY: The ratification of the Washington Conference Treaties is a subject that hasn't been dealt with very much. We have a book (*The Politics of Arms Control Treaty Ratification*) coming out next month—seven of us did one together—in which we looked at all of the arms control treaties, the recent ones as well as the older ones. There were two historians and five political scientists

---

Presented in a Forum at the Miller Center of Public Affairs on 1 November 1991.

writing this book. Strangely enough, we had different views as to what was important and what was unimportant. The historians felt that the contents of the treaties were most important. The political scientists felt that how the president operated was most important. I don't think a single political scientist listed the contents of the treaty as one of his five most important aspects of the treaties. They listed manipulation and politics. I am going to talk about some of the politics of Warren G. Harding.

On 11 November 1921, President Warren G. Harding provided a colorful ceremony in Arlington Cemetery at the burial of America's Unknown Soldier. The next day the Washington Conference on the Limitation of Armaments began. Harding gave one of his speeches, which he called "bloviations," a marvelous word for political speech. Harding could bloviate all over when he got rolling!

Harding made this speech, one word tumbling after another—a typical welcoming speech. Most people thought that Secretary of State Charles Evans Hughes would make the same kind of speech and perhaps tell where the bar and the party was, which is typical of the first day of every convention sort of speech. He stunned everyone by listing 845,000 tons of warships—15 battleships and battle cruisers under construction and 15 existing battleships—that the United States would consider scrapping. The Japanese and the British clapped like mad—"Those crazy Americans have done it again!"

Hughes then asked the British to stop construction or scrap a total of 23 ships—583,000 tons of ships. One British admiral leaned forward in his chair and reacted in the manner of a bulldog who had been poked in the stomach by the unwary foot of a traveling salesman, because nobody did that to the British Royal Navy.

Hughes then proposed that the Japanese scrap 448,000 tons of ships by stopping construction on six capital ships and by scrapping 17 others. Hughes, in about half an hour, sank 76 ships, more than all the admirals of the world had done in the previous century. Admirals don't like to lose battleships. It's one of their tendencies that we are all aware of. Hughes then called for a ten-year naval holiday in the construction of capital ships and for a ratio of 5:5:3, 525,000 tons for the United States, 525,000 tons for Great Britain, and 315,000 tons for Japan. He later suggested 167,000 tons for the French and the Italians. The Italians really didn't care how many tons they got, whether it was zero or a million, as long as it was the same as France.

Hughes, in perhaps the most dramatic proposal ever made by an American diplomat, had played his trump card at the very beginning of the conference. He captured the attention of America and the world. The *New York Evening Post* rejoiced that "Hughes has injected into the work of international understanding and peace that touch of audacity, almost of ruthlessness, which has hitherto been associated with the business of war." He hit home with a great many people.

Difficult negotiations followed with the Japanese, who wanted a higher ratio because they had figured out in 1907 or so that they needed a 70-percent ratio over any other power attempting to dominate the seas near Japan. The Japanese also wanted a clause prohibiting the further fortification of Pacific islands, a defensive clause once again. It's always termed a defensive clause. The French forced exclusion of all auxiliary ships—cruisers, destroyers, and submarines—from coverage. The French, as always, complicated things.

Providing for the scrapping of 71 ships, the Five-Power Naval Limitation Treaty imposed a ten-year naval holiday on the construction of capital ships, set up the ratio described above and stipulated no further fortification of Pacific islands: for the United States, this included the Philippines, Guam, and Wake (but not Hawaii); for the Japanese, this included Formosa, the Pescadores, and several other islands around Japan.

There was another open session of the Washington Conference that dealt with Pacific and Asian issues. Many of the delegates expected Hughes to make a similar comprehensive proposal on naval armaments in the Pacific. All of these people were relieved beyond expression when Hughes ended up talking very little about the Pacific.

There were five other conference treaties. The only key one for our ratification story is the Four-Power Pact, which dealt with the Pacific: the United States, Great Britain, France, and Japan. This ended the Anglo-Japanese Alliance, which the United States in particular felt was directed against it. The treaty also provided that the four powers would jointly confer if disputes arose among them or if aggression came about in the Pacific area.

The Four-Power Pact is important to remember because it, and not the Five-Power Naval Limitation Treaty, became the center of the Senate ratification struggle. The task of getting the treaties through the Senate fell to Henry Cabot Lodge. The wisdom of appointing Lodge to the delegation became apparent during the ratification debate. Lodge handled his task with experience and skill. It is important to emphasize the cooperation of Oscar W. Underwood. Lodge was the head of the Republican party in the Senate; Underwood was the head of the Democratic party, and he cooperated.

The Cabinet was unimportant. They did little active politicking with senators themselves. The major numerical opposition, after all, was composed of Democrats, not overly susceptible to Republican blandishments. (Things haven't changed.) In addition, no one really expected Republicans like William E. Borah and Hiram Johnson to vote in favor of the treaties, but strangely enough, with the exception of the Four-Power Pact, they did.

Hughes worked on the senators through the press, but the key figure in the Senate was Lodge. The senior senator from Massachusetts was entering the twilight of his career and of his life in 1921 and 1922. He was the Senate majority leader, chairman of the Senate Foreign Relations Committee, and in many respects, the leader of the Republican party. He had worked hard to elect Harding president. His closeness to Harding was a great source of power, every bit as important as his senatorial positions. Respected and even feared by some of the fledgling Republican senators, one could not say he was loved or popular within his own party—not at all.

Democrats hated him with a vengeance. One of these, Senator John Williams of Mississippi, bragged that he had never agreed with Lodge, and hoped that he would die before such a catastrophe ever occurred. Democrats threw many bitter and hateful words at Lodge during the ratification debates. Some were even his own words. The opposition delighted in citing speeches Lodge had made against the League in 1919 and 1920, which they now resurrected to use against Lodge in the treaties he was presenting.

Lodge demonstrated no public uneasiness at his change in position, but he periodically took a leave of absence when the debate got hard. He would simply walk out before he would say anything. While he won no friends in the Senate, he performed brilliantly in the ratification struggle.

Oscar W. Underwood gave the Harding administration great strength in this struggle. He was a personal friend of Harding's when the Ohio politician served in the Senate. The Alabama Democrat had offered to resign as Minority Leader when Harding appointed him to the American delegation. Several leading Democrats, William Gibbs McAdoo in particular, called upon him to do so. The party failed to take a position, and he remained. Underwood said, "The President and I are not playing party politics. We are out of the three-mile limit and are fighting the battles of American democracy." He played an active role at the conference in the Chinese Customs Treaty, but did little in the Five-Power Naval Limitation Treaty.

During the ratification debates, Democrats accused him of ignoring the Democrats who opposed the treaty and spending all his time with Lodge and Harding, which was indeed true. He spent an enormous amount of time with Lodge and Harding. Underwood defended himself in a three-hour speech on the Senate floor. Hughes later wrote him, "I have never known a finer illustration of a nonpartisan statesmanship." Harvard University gave him an honorary doctor of laws degree as a result of his work on the delegation. Later he was offered a position on the Supreme Court by Harding but declined. Underwood certainly hurt his credibility as minority leader among his colleagues, and he resigned from that position in 1923.

Executive-congressional relationships were not positive during the entire process of the Washington treaties. The results of the 1920 election had changed the narrow senatorial margin of 49 Republicans and 47 Democrats in 1919 to 59 Republicans and 37 Democrats in 1921. Harding had far more strength in the Senate after the 1920 election and was in a far better position than Woodrow Wilson had been in.

As a senator, Harding had not made many enemies. His performance as president had not yet created divisive camps. They hadn't quite figured out Harding yet; he was still something of a mystery, which was fortunate for Hughes and the Republicans. Two years later Harding would have been a millstone around the Republicans' neck.

The Senate Foreign Relations Committee had ten Republicans and six Democrats in 1921. Lodge was the chairman. He made sure that new members agreed with his foreign policy before he appointed them to the committee. With such strong majorities, the constitutional requirement for a two-thirds vote played no part whatsoever in the Naval Limitation Treaty, and only a small role in the Four-Power Pact that dealt with the Pacific. If the Republicans remained cohesive and followed Lodge, Harding would need just five Democratic votes. Lodge's task was to make sure that only a few Republicans would join Borah and that Underwood would deliver enough Democrats to offset these desertions.

The fight against the treaties was led by Senator William Borah, who was the wild man of the Senate in the 1920s and 1930s. He looked like John L. Lewis—bushy hair, bushy eyebrows, and a great orator. To my great surprise and after studying the man for years, a new book last year said that he had a lifelong love affair with Alice Roosevelt. That stuns me, because I would not have thought William Borah would have been interested in that sort of thing.

Hiram Johnson, Robert M. La Follette, James Reed of Missouri, and Joseph Robinson all had voted against the League of Nations. Almost all of the remaining irreconcilables still in the Senate voted against the Four-Power Pact. None, however, with the exception of Senator France of Maryland, a Republican, voted against the Naval Limitation Treaty. The lone vote by a non-irreconcilable against the Chinese Customs Treaty was the only other vote cast against any of the treaties except for the Four-Power Pact.

The Harding administration worked hard to prevent a major split within the Republican ranks. Hiram Johnson was furious with Harding. He wrote, "Harding was seeking in every possible way to unite every possible element. He wants to move smoothly along the path of least resistance, and in order to do so, I think, will make to us, as well as to others, all sorts of concessions."

Borah and La Follette did vote in favor of the Five-Power Naval Limitation Treaty. Johnson did not cast a vote. The irreconcilable Republicans did not attract any other Republicans to their side. Many Democrats gleefully joined them in the Four-Power Pact, but only one voted against the Five-Power Naval Limitation Treaty, whose enormous popularity prevented it from splitting the Republican party or becoming a partisan issue.

Often overlooked is that the 1920 election was the greatest victory in American electoral history up to that time. Harding won over 60 percent of the popular vote. That election combined with retirements and deaths brought 23 new senators to the ratification debates in 1922, almost one-fourth of the Senate. Eighteen Republicans and five Democrats made up the freshman class.

Led by Lodge and conscious of Harding's popularity, the Republicans followed the party line in such an astonishing degree that not a single new Republican cast a vote against any of the six treaties that came before the Senate. Only two got out of their chairs to make speeches during the senatorial debates. Lodge had them in his pocket. Four of the five new Democrats, on the other hand, argued strongly and voted against several of the treaties, although one of them from Louisiana voted for all of the treaties.

Harding and his colleagues also handled the Navy with great skill. They made it clear, and this is an important point, that arms treaties were political questions to be decided on the basis of political considerations. Military considerations fell into a secondary category. Therefore, military advice to the Washington Conference did not become a major determinant of policy. During the Senate ratification, Lodge said:

> It is not for technical experts to make this treaty any more than I regard it as a duty of technical experts to make the Tariff Bill. The idea should be dismissed that the naval experts were to formulate the policy to be pursued or that we should ever have allowed them to do it. The policy, be it good or bad, was the policy of the

government represented by the American delegates at the Conference.

To open the Senate debate, the administration brought out its chief asset, President Harding, who was still basking in the honeymoon glow of his great election victory. He appeared personally before the Senate and asked for the overwhelming support of all the treaties. Almost in Wilsonian terms, he said, "We shall discredit the influence of the Republic, render future efforts futile or unlikely, and write discouragement where today the world is ready to claim new hope if we don't approve these treaties." No one would ever have accused Harding of talking like Wilson, but that is exactly what he was doing at this time.

Lodge ran a blitzkrieg campaign. As the Senate majority leader, he greatly influenced the Senate calendar and thus set the pace for treaty ratification. He presented the treaties to the Senate Foreign Relations Committee on 10 February. By 17 February, all the treaties got a favorable report by unanimous votes from the Senate Foreign Relations Committee. Only at one meeting was the Five-Power Naval Limitation Treaty ever discussed, and then only briefly. At all other meetings the opponents of the Four-Power Pact sought more information from the government. The final result was a reservation stating that the Four-Power Pact was not an alliance. *Alliance* was the key word. They looked it up in Webster's Dictionary; they looked at everything but history books to see what the definition of an alliance was. They didn't quite trust historians at this stage.

Most amazingly, not a single hearing on any of the treaties was held. Not a single witness, either in favor of or opposed to any of the treaties, ever got the opportunity to testify. As a newspaper writer commented, "The great difference between the Four-Power Pact and the League Covenant is that one was of Republican origin and the other was of Democratic origin."

The process stood in stark contrast with the League debates two years before. Committee records indicate no dissent to these procedures, but several Democratic senators in a full debate on the Senate floor indicated that they favored having naval experts testify on the Naval Treaty. That it did not happen is an indication of the weakness of the opposition and the strength of Harding and Lodge.

It is difficult to believe from the perspective of 1991 that any arms control treaty, no matter how popular in this age of congressional scrutiny, could escape congressional hearings.

The steamroller continued at high speed when the treaties came before the full Senate. Senators found their mail stuffed with letters and petitions from virtually every organized church, women, pacifist, and pro-arms control group in the country, calling for the ratification of the Five-Power Naval Limitation Treaty. There were approximately 11 million letters received in a few months, and most of them mentioned religion in one way or another. It was a very highly organized support program.

Almost all the debate was on the Four-Power Pact. Harding and Lodge insisted that the defeat of the Four-Power Pact would lead to the defeat of the Naval Treaty, and they deliberately tied the two treaties together. Whether in fact it would have made a great deal of difference is extremely controversial. Lodge kept the treaties constantly before the United States Senate, so much so that opposition senators on both sides complained about the pressure. He wouldn't let them talk about anything else; the treaties were constantly there.

Many remembered how slow Lodge had been in the League debates; he stalled, very carefully, slowly investigating everything. He was constantly reminded of this by all the Democrats. Lodge ignored them, went on, and brushed aside these protests. Everyone recognized Lodge's strategy, but he had the troops and his opponents didn't. They had little recourse as Lodge struck at the peak of public support and the crest of a popular president's power. Since Harding is usually ranked very near the bottom of the presidential polls today, many of us forget how extremely popular he was during the election and for about a year afterwards. It was during that particular time that the Washington Conference Treaty was put through.

Americans were extremely proud that the treaty was negotiated in Washington, D.C. A newspaper said: "Here was a small, unsophisticated American provincial capital that had great honesty in comparison to Paris and London and these other dens of iniquity that were across the Atlantic Ocean." My, how times have changed.

On the question of safeguards, the conference delegates relied on "good faith," the belief that they and their countries were all honorable. Trust was the key word, and with it, no verification measures were necessary in the treaties. After all, who could hide the construction of a battleship? Indeed, that feat is difficult, but it is possible to hide the details, such as gun elevations and additional tonnage. The Japanese, in particular, had a systematic program of adding 2,000 or 3,000 more tons to almost every vessel during the interwar period. A minor recordage requirement on the construction of replacement tonnage did not include any method to verify the accuracy of reported information. You simply asked the other side what they were doing. They told you, and no one checked to see if it was true.

Not a single senator suggested safeguards. To the eyes of arms controllers in 1991, when little international trust appears to exist, such naiveté is almost shocking. But the 1920s was an age of idealism and trust that only the harsh realities of the 1930s and 1940s destroyed.

Senatorial support for the Five-Power Naval Limitation Treaty allowed Republicans to combine popular support of arms limitation with party regularity. Who could resist under those particular circumstances? The only Republican vote cast against the Naval Limitation Treaty—by Senator France—came largely as a result of his distrust of the British.

We forget that quite a number of senators at this time actually distrusted the British more than the Japanese. Senator France felt we were better off if we had a large navy. He was from Maryland, which built naval ships, so his political philosophy and principle were compatible with his interests. James Reed of Missouri would have voted against the treaty, but he wasn't there. He was an enormously stubborn man, and for his entire political career he was against all kinds of proposals. It would appear he would not have hesitated to vote against the Naval Limitation Treaty if the entire state of Missouri had favored it. He felt strongly about this. Borah was that way on occasion. Borah would make a public announcement that he did not care if every single person in Idaho opposed something; he was going to vote for it. This is representative government working at its best.

Other doubters kept their opinions to themselves, and until further evidence surfaces, it appears amazingly that almost every senator did favor the Naval Limitation Treaty. The timing was perfect: a combination of an immediate postwar period and no serious threats of war among the major naval powers. There were a few books around on both sides already talking about war between the United States and Japan. Hector Bywater, the British naval expert, was to publish one shortly. Several Japanese books had already appeared. But no one was paying a great deal of attention to those types of books, which have started to appear once again.

Harding and Hughes deliberately sought limited goals, and until they actually carried out their negotiations, did make the mistake of promising more than they could actually achieve. They feared failure and were thus willing to settle for less, to take a few steps toward peace, rather than leaping into unknown waters as Woodrow Wilson had done. Unfortunately, they later marred their record by claiming too much. Once the conference was over, they claimed that perpetual peace was here forever. It didn't quite work out that way.

Hughes' dramatic presentation at the opening of the conference was brilliantly done, as both a negotiating and public relations stroke. Only 11 people knew what was going to be proposed. (This was before the photocopy machine.)

Hughes did have some advantages at the conference. One of them was Herbert Osborne Yardley, a gentleman about whom I am writing a biography. Yardley, an American code cracker, had cracked the Japanese code, and he was laying the Japanese messages on Hughes' desk each morning before the negotiations. Hughes knew exactly what the Japanese were going to propose before they proposed it. Yardley is a fascinating character.

It was a clear, simple proposal that Americans could understand: scrapping battleships. Thus, the treaty appeared fairly simple, but it actually was much more complex. All of its implications were not clearly thought out. Many of the original proposals were not carried out. There were no verification inspection provisions. There were loopholes big enough to steam a heavy cruiser through, which is exactly what did steam through.

These loopholes did not surface until well after the negotiation and ratification of the treaty, and in particular, the naval officers were kept quiet, in part because Secretary of the Navy Edwin Denby deserted them. The assistant secretary of the Navy, Theodore Roosevelt, Jr., played a key role. The Navy was deserted by its leadership, so all the problems were in the future.

The Harding administration also made a major strategic decision, in my opinion, when it tied all the treaties together in one political-military package. It used the enormous popularity of the Naval Limitation Treaty to carry the others through, but during the conference and ratification, the United States had indicated clearly to both Great Britain and to Japan that the United States would not ratify the Naval Limitation Treaty unless all of the other treaties were ratified. The Japanese would have to give up the Anglo-Japanese Alliance, an enormously important alliance to them. Some Englishmen today still argue that if that treaty had not been given up, the British would have been able to restrain the Japanese, and the Second World War would not have occurred in the way it did. Japan also agreed to leave Shantung and Siberia. Thus, there were all sorts of political implications tied into these treaties.

The decision to tie the Naval Limitation Treaty to political arrangements was the major decision of the conference and made the Naval Limitation Treaty and the other treaties possible. My argument is that the most successful arms control treaties are not the ones standing out there all by themselves but the ones that are tied together with political arrangements.

Lodge, with malice aforethought, pushed the treaties through the Senate and did not schedule the vote on the Five-Power Naval Limitation Treaty until after the votes on the other controversial treaties. He had it set up beautifully. Almost all the public supporters of the Naval Limitation Treaty fell into line and demanded the ratification of all the treaties. Lodge did this with the Four-Power Pact in particular. Whether he actually designed it to happen this way, I don't know. I'm still not sure that he expected the argument over the Four-Power Pact that occurred.

Hughes wrote a few years later that the main American achievement was that for the next 15 years we should not do what everyone knew we would not do: not build capital ships or fortify Pacific islands. It was very clear to Hughes that the Republican Congress of the 1920s didn't want to vote money for anything, let alone for battleships or fortifying Pacific islands.

Harding stated, on the other hand, that if these treaties were ratified by the Senate, then his administration's name would be secure in history. In fact, it is almost the only positive event secured by the Harding administration for the history books.

In the history of 20th century arms limitation, if politics is indeed the art of the possible, then the Washington Naval Conference of 1921 and 1922 represents the peak of political impressionism. Bold in conception, a daring break with the past, its originators hoped to establish a model for the restriction of weapons that future statesmen could emulate. Bright but powerful facets of domestic and international politics flowed together on the canvas in a form that captured momentary reality and reflected the hopes and ambiguities that have always marked the pursuit of arms control.

Repetition, however, of this stunning, unforgettable drama proved unattainable. One reviewer, 45 years later, wrote that "unlike SALT, the Washington Conference involved serious arms reduction. Indeed, it is the only historical example of reductions of this magnitude." Later imitators might have forgotten or ignored the achievements of the Washington Conference, but they failed to understand the foundation of political craftsmanship that made the success of the conference possible.

QUESTION: To what extent did the limitation in the 1925 treaty help or hurt us in the 1930s when we had to re-arm?

MR. BUCKLEY: There are people who believe that the Washington Conference was an absolutely horrible mistake and that it set us up for the Japanese in 1941. Those critics should look at the other side of the argument: No treaty is forever. Any treaty established like this is for a short period of time. Arms control treaties, because they are far more specific than regular political treaties, are susceptible to breaking down.

Second, the real mistake came after the conference. We failed to build even the ships that we were allowed. In a period of—and this figure may not be exactly right—18 years, for eight of those 18 years the United States built no ships and the Japanese built from two to four every single year. When you do not build up to your own treaty, there is a real problem.

The treaties did end in 1936. Even then we hesitated, for example, to build up naval bases. We feared that pouring money into Guam would be such a provocation to the Japanese that it would push the Japanese earlier, rather than later, into attacking the United States.

The big question that no one has answered yet is whether it saved any money. This is one of the things I'm trying to figure out. One of the great arguments in favor of arms control is that in fact you do save money. I don't believe we did when you consider what we had to build later at higher rates, but I am not prepared to make a specific conclusion on that yet because it is a difficult question to figure.

To me it is key that we got a better relative position by not building. We got a 5:5:3 ratio, which is really the same as a 10:10:6, during this 15-year period. Had all three nations continued to build, that ratio would have been ten for the United States, eleven for Great Britain, and nine for Japan. I would argue that during that 15-year period, if one believes that those ships were actually going to be built, we would actually have had a better relative position. It seems to me that there are arguments on both sides of this particular question.

NARRATOR: What about the argument that it would legitimize for the world Japan's right to build up to this level? She could have built to nine without the treaty, but it wouldn't have been legitimized.

MR. BUCKLEY: Japan had basically been recognized as a great power by the Anglo-Japanese Alliance of 1902, and it seems to me that the legitimacy of Japan's position was already there. Japan controlled the western Pacific before the conference began, for all practical purposes. The United States Navy was not strong enough to go across the Pacific and defeat the Japanese.

A combination of the United States and Great Britain might have been able to defeat Japan, since the Japanese would be fighting from short mileage. Still, many believed that there would be a great naval battle. The United States would sail its fleet across the Pacific, and somewhere around the Philippines, the Japanese, as they had done in the Russo-Japanese war, would attack the United States fleet and defeat it. Even Admiral Yamamoto thought that as late as the Battle of Midway, because one of the purposes of it was to get those U.S. aircraft carriers and to draw the rest of them into the battle.

Japan had already achieved a legitimate desire and demonstrated some need. The only question was about the number the Japanese wanted: the 10:10:7 rather than the 10:10:6. We are only talking about one battleship, which was not going to change the whole character of the strategic balance.

As you know, there were great divisions within the Japanese navy and within the Japanese government between the naval ministers who were admirals and tended to be like Prime Minister Kato—men who put the needs of the state before those of the navy. The other Kato, Admiral Kato, pushed the navy first. For about the first ten years, the navy minister, who unfortunately died, and his followers pretty much successfully kept the treaties. After the London Conference, however, Admiral Kato and his supporters came forward and seized the initiative. It seems to me that Japan was a legitimate naval power in its time.

QUESTION: You emphasized the technique of the administration and the Senate majority leader. I wonder whether that isn't a mistake of emphasis and that the real lesson to be found in studying these events is that technique doesn't matter too much. It is the underlying substantive world situation that makes arms treaties possible. I have studied this period a great deal, but I wouldn't have thought to read the debates on this because it seems to me that the treaty was set up before they got to Washington, and that it is implicit in the situation.

When you emphasize Hughes' skill, Harding's good will, and Henry Cabot Lodge's skillful manipulation of the Senate, aren't you looking at side issues? What you have done is paint a wonderful picture for us, but isn't it the essence of the problem that we should look at if we are interested in lessons for arms control?

MR. BUCKLEY: I'm not stressing the negotiations and background. I am stressing only the ratification part, not what took place before.

Second, I'm not as sure as you are that what happened was "as inevitable" as you suggest. Nor am I as certain that the British government did not desire for a lot of reasons to keep the Anglo-Japanese alliance. Many people within the British government did not want to be pressured. You read this especially in the messages from the Foreign Office to Tokyo at this time.

COMMENT: Some people foresaw after the Japanese invasion of Manchuria a war between Japan and the United States. They never anticipated a European war.

MR. BUCKLEY: There is a magnificent book that has just come out by the cultural editor of the *New York Times*, a man named Honan. He has just written a book on Hector Bywater.

Hector Bywater was a British naval expert and a fascinating man. He was a spy for Great Britain against the Germans. He wrote a book in 1925 called *The Great Pacific War*. This book designs basically how the war would occur in 1931 and 1932. He does everything but predict the Pearl Harbor attack, and he couldn't have done that because the American fleet wasn't yet stationed at Pearl Harbor.

Homer Lea had written a book like this called *The Ignorance of Valor* some 20 years before. Supposedly, Admiral Yamamoto read Bywater's book, met with him for discussion, and got his ideas for the Pearl Harbor attack from Bywater. I think Mr. Honan is going a little far in that particular theory, especially when on the last page he has Yamamoto ordering the assassination of Bywater in 1940. Most of the book is pretty good, however. What you suggest was indeed there long before 1930.

There were various politicians in the United States who really believed this. In my home state of Indiana, a friend of mine did a doctoral dissertation on public opinion there for a period from 1914 to 1920. In this midwestern farm state in which there were fewer than 25 Japanese, during the period 1914 to 1920, they rated Japan as the number one enemy in the world. They would have rather fought Japan than Germany. There were strong feelings largely based on a lot of ignorance at that particular time which developed quite early.

Clearly, Japan was going to be a threat. It depended on what Japan did, and, of course, at the Washington Conference, they backed off. It is the only time in the period before the Second World War when they pulled Japanese troops out of some place as a result of the conference—Shantung, Siberia—places of this sort.

NARRATOR: You mentioned the word *idealism* as related to the acceptance. Doesn't this run in the face of the Senate's action on the League? Can you tell us about what seems to be a revisionist body of thought concerning Lodge's and Wilson's failure to do anything about enlisting the political skills that you described Lodge using in this episode?

Further, can you say anything about the argument that seems to be going on in some places that Lodge was more right than Wilson on the League? If he was more right, was it for idealistic reasons, or did he simply understand as a realist what American national interests and the restraints on America were?

MR. BUCKLEY: Both those words are unfortunately like *liberal* and *conservative*: They have many shades of meaning. There clearly was an enormous belief in the 1920s, on the power of public opinion, that if only people would rise up and want peace, peace would be secure. It seems to me the Kellogg-Briand Pact is one of the classic examples. Also, these disarmament treaties have a strong measure of belief that public opinion could solve things. E. H. Carr in his work on international relations between the wars talks a lot about this public opinion facet. It was extremely powerful and idealistic. Simply by outlawing war, war would cease. In their opinion, arms, in fact, caused war. It was a convenient opinion because we weren't going to build the ships and put soldiers in the Army anyway because Congress was simply not prepared to spend that money.

There is an argument on the second point, which Roland Stromberg in particular has argued, that collective security is an idea whose time will never come, because not only was Wilson wrong, but the ideas of collective security behind both the League and the United Nations are wrong. In his opinion the essence of collective security is a flawed concept. He's probably got the clearest book of the dozens written along this particular line.

Wilson remains controversial. We have all these things he wrote. I can't even begin to estimate how much material Woodrow Wilson wrote, but compared to Franklin Roosevelt, Wilson ought to be very clear. He attracts historians who in large part have made up their minds before they look at the materials on how they are going to fit him into one of these idealist or realist models. Then they produce the book. It seems to me there is still much work to be done on Wilson. In some ways he remains mysterious as to his philosophy.

The argument of Arthur Link, my old professor, is that Wilson's idealism is not so much an idealism but a higher realism. He becomes more and more favorable to Wilson with each passing year.

COMMENT: When you read the Lodge papers, you find that he is a realist but within cautious limits. He is prepared to accept a certain international role for America. It is surprising in light of the clarity of the evidence that the interwar literature is as anti-Lodge as it is.

MR. BUCKLEY: William C. Widener wrote the Versailles Treaty chapter in our book that will soon be out, and obviously he would agree 100 percent with what you are saying. Let's suppose the League had passed the Senate with reservations. Remember that ratification is with the advice and consent of the Senate, but the final legal act is the presidential act. Would Woodrow Wilson have signed? I have serious doubts as to whether he would have. He was so committed by that particular time, and legally he did not have to do so. He could have killed his own baby, you know, in a manner much stronger than even Thomas A. Bailey suggested in his books.

QUESTION: It seems to me that the battleship is a better weapon to confront commercial shipping than it is to confront other battleships. In the Battle of Jutland they spent a lot of time running away from each other. Is this treaty a means to make the battleship obsolete as a weapon? If so, does that mean that any reasonable or viable arms control process should have limits on arms by ratio as a means to make that arms or that weapon system obsolete?

MR. BUCKLEY: Actually, a battleship is not particularly that good for commercial warfare. Some critics argue that the battleship was a dead weapon in 1920 and 1921 already, and that Pearl Harbor only confirmed it.

Submarines are a lot better for attacking commercial shipping, and they were a definite issue for that reason at the conferences. Submarines continued to be free of any limits. Aircraft carriers were limited in size (total tonnage) but not in terms of total numbers. In fact, the United States was able to change two of its uncompleted battleships into aircraft carriers. The history of the aircraft carrier still hasn't been studied carefully enough. Here is a major weapon system that developed almost overnight, in the 1920s and 1930s, compared to the way navies usually develop. I'm still not sure we understand exactly how it happened.

COMMENT: Politicians know how to write treaties and lose wars, but they don't know how to win. The treaty limited battleships and perhaps cruisers, which was certainly not the key to winning in the Pacific in 1941. They played a minor role. Perhaps the same goes for arms reduction today, having nothing to do with what might go on in the future. Everybody is willing to kill SDI without knowing whether it might be another "flattop" that will revolutionize warfare.

MR. BUCKLEY: I think arms control at particular times and in particular places is useful and valuable. It cannot carry the whole

149

burden of relationships between nations. The treaties are too vulnerable.

COMMENT: It cannot be done in a vacuum with politicians only and without the expert advice of military personnel. They have to work together.

MR. BUCKLEY: There has to be a working relationship. At the Geneva Conference in 1927 they had military delegates and left most of the politicians at home. The result was that military men were beating each other over the head and nothing happened. One could make an argument that you can't do one or the other; you have to have a good combination. Good arms control treaties are hard to do.

QUESTION: And in this day and age, how long are they relevant? Something else comes down the pike and you may find that you have limited the wrong device!

MR. BUCKLEY: I would admit that today there is a possibility of that happening. I would argue that arms control treaties are made for political reasons. They are not made in the belief that they are going to prevent more war or bring a better peace or any of these altruistic reasons. They are made because one nation thinks it is going to gain some sort of advantage in that treaty. I believe that strongly. I don't care what the politicians are saying in public, and the Washington Conference is a good example of that. They constantly talked to the public about peace, but they actually were interested in other things.

NARRATOR: Thank you for a most enlightening discussion. We will remember Washington Conference Treaties when we think about other arms agreements.

IV.

NUCLEAR WEAPONS COMPLEXITIES

CHAPTER EIGHT

Nuclear Weapons Complexes in the Post–Cold War World: Lessons From the Soviet Case*

GEORGE PERKOVICH

NARRATOR: "It seems to me," writes George Perkovich of the W. Alton Jones Foundation, "that we are at a moment when integrative and disintegrative forces are tugging at the world with near equal strength, confronting leaders with a fundamental choice, 'Which side do you pull?'" I thought when I read his statement that it provides insight into Mr. Perkovich's career. There are two traditions in private foundations. One is the great tradition of professionalism. The other tradition is that of anonymity—being behind the scenes, being virtually invisible, wearing grey flannel suits. The second tradition has its merits, but some of us would come down on the side of the former tradition. Mr. Perkovich seems to fit that former mold.

George Perkovich is the director of the Secure Society Program of the W. Alton Jones Foundation and manages the foundation's large grant-making budget. He designs, initiates, and implements ideas for furthering the foundation board's mandate of reducing the risk of nuclear war.

---

*Presented in a Forum at the Miller Center on 6 March 1992.

In an earlier incarnation, he served as a fellow of the World Policy Institute, was a foreign policy adviser and speech writer to a U.S. senator, and was the executive director of the International Student Pugwash, a nonprofit organization that conducts education on the social impacts of science and technology.

Mr. Perkovich's writings appear in dozens of publications: the *Atlantic Monthly, Foreign Policy*, the *Bulletin of Atomic Scientists*, the *New York Times*, and the *Christian Science Monitor*. He is the author of *Defending Europe Without Nuclear Weapons*. We are particularly anxious to hear his discussion.

MR. PERKOVICH: We sit here today in this beautiful building 50 years after the largest scientific and engineering complex ever established was created to produce the first nuclear weapon. It is one of those instances where you can't tell if 50 years is a long or short time, but it appears that it is *enough* time to cause a fundamental breakdown in the U.S. and Soviet nuclear weapons complexes. Indeed, we can see that there is a breakdown in the overall physical and intellectual apparatus of the nuclear weapons establishments. I want to discuss the extent of this breakdown, the dangers and uncertainties that arise from the collapsing physical and intellectual infrastructures of the nuclear weapons complexes, and then discuss what possibly can be done about it.

Several questions are at the core of what I think is happening here. First, how do we nationally and internationally manage the extremely costly and environmentally sensitive task of decommissioning and dismantling the physical apparatus of nuclear weapons complexes?

Second, what can the international community do to protect against the dangers resulting from instability and change of ownership of nuclear weapons complexes? This is an acute problem in Russia today. It may also occur in North Korea where a regime change is perhaps in the offing. India also is a potential problem area. I heard a joke a while ago about Scotland taking over the Sellafield plutonium reprocessing facilities when it becomes independent of England. These changes of ownership of nuclear weapons complexes pose problems that haven't been confronted in the past. Within this category, there is also a risk of the spread of

154

fissile materials or the transfer of weapons capabilities to desperate regimes or factions within a country.

Finally, what do we do, both nationally and internationally, about the scientists and engineers who know how to make nuclear weapons and may find themselves unemployed and tempted by aspiring proliferators? Are there things we can do to protect ourselves against this potential problem? In essence, the question is, what kind of strategy and plan is necessary to build *down* the nuclear establishments that have been built up over the last 50 years?

In addressing this question, I find myself being led full circle to an analysis that Robert Oppenheimer and others made at the beginning of the nuclear age. The concept needs to be remodeled to reflect what we have learned in the changing situations, but I believe the basic idea must be confronted head on: the need for a comprehensive international approach to managing nuclear weapons materials and the establishments capable of producing them.

This concept raises at least two large subsidiary questions. First, what does international control of these establishments mean? Does it mean physical possession by an international entity, or can it mean something else? Second, does this notion of control require international control of nuclear weapons themselves, or can they remain in the possession of nation-states?

This is a great deal to talk about in a brief moment of time. On much of this I am at the stage of identifying an agenda for future work and trying to identify other people who are working in this direction to create a critical mass that can push this agenda forward.

Where are we today? In ways that nuclear strategists and others in the national security establishment still do not recognize, the Cold War ended just in time. It may be coincidental or one of those historical ironies, but the political and strategic "fuel" of the East-West conflict ran out at the same time that the nuclear reactors which turned this fuel into weapons started breaking down. It is underappreciated, but true nonetheless. Within the last few years, reactors have had to be closed for environmental and safety reasons, just as the Berlin Wall collapsed and the political fuel for this race lost all of its rationale.

155

We are now at the point where leading figures such as Congressman Les Aspin (D-Wis.), chairman of the House Armed Services Committee, said in a draft of a nuclear strategy document that he has been circulating, "If offered a magic wand to eradicate the existence and knowledge of nuclear weapons, we would accept it." This is a different position from one he would have taken two years ago. His view of nuclear weapons used to be that they were the equalizer for, in our case, Soviet conventional superiority. Today he says in effect that we are the "equalizee," and so we are better off eliminating all nuclear weapons if we can.

What Aspin and others still haven't recognized is the damage that nuclear weapons production did to the domestic health of the producer countries. This also was a failure of strategists. For decades the national security establishment and arms controllers have focused on avoiding the use of nuclear weapons. The weapons were considered dangerous only if they were exploded in a conflict. Now, however, we know that to be not entirely true. The act of producing the weapons is itself dangerous, and it has caused lasting harm to the countries in which the production occurred.

This harm takes several forms. Environmentally, the damage is beginning to be appreciated. For example, at Hanford in Washington, which produced most of the plutonium, the contaminated liquid waste that was dumped into the ground there would fill railroad cars stretching 16,500 miles. Over 440 billion gallons of contaminated waste was dumped into the soil there. The Governmental Affairs Committee in the Senate has just concluded that to dismantle our nuclear weapons complex as now planned would require decontaminating 7,000 buildings in 20 states at a cost of over $300 billion.

The health effects of atmospheric testing and the subsequent effect of radiation on human beings have been calculated using U.N. standards, and the calculations indicate that there will be over 430,000 additional cancer deaths in the next 40 years due to atmospheric testing. Furthermore, there are studies to determine the effects on employees working in this complex. Such tests, however, were not conducted in the past because the DOE until the last couple of years refused to release the data. We are funding a group, for example, that is determining the accuracy and completeness of the data. The early indications are that the data are very unreliable, so there may be much more danger inherent in working in these facilities than previously has been understood.

In the Russian nuclear weapons complex around Chelyabinsk, there is a working assumption that at least 4,000 workers were killed in a 1957 explosion. Downriver, whole communities have been abandoned due to the effects of open dumping of radioactive waste into the rivers.

The effects of secrecy on the functioning of democratic process, impaired by the nuclear weapons complex, are now coming out. The DOE is still the most difficult agency from which to get Freedom of Information Act requests fulfilled—we don't have the data. We have documents from the CIA and the Department of Defense, yet there is almost no documentation on what DOE has done over the years.

There is also the fiscal damage done by the nuclear weapons complex. The weapons complex operated on an annual budget of tens of billions of dollars, but now we have to include cleanup costs, which will be at least $300 billion.

The important thing is that such damage happened not just in the United States and the Soviet Union. Great environmental damage has also occurred in Britain around the Sellafield plutonium reprocessing facilities. In France there are some investigations now underway to determine what harmful effects occurred there. In Israel a law was changed last year to enable workers at the Dimona complex to sue the government for injuries suffered working there, and that process is now beginning to reveal contamination around Dimona. In China, at a conference Chinese nuclear scientists assured everyone that they, in fact, had none of these problems, and that all the problems the United States and Russia had were special to the United States and Russia. I am willing to guess that this will prove not to be the case. The point is that this is an international phenomena—anywhere there is a nuclear weapons complex, there are these domestic harms.

I would argue this is important, because when the information on the full range of domestic ills caused by weapons production is publicized, it should provide a clear lesson for why countries considering entering into the nuclear weapons business should think twice. It is not a cost-free endeavor in any sense of the word. Secondly, publication of these domestic ill effects also gives ammunition to constituencies in other countries, ammunition to challenge their governments over what may be secret or semi-open nuclear weapons facilities. A worldwide democratic movement to stop this activity is fomented once this information is released. Third, in starting to discuss the huge waste management and cleanup challenges, one can begin to identify alternative career paths not only for current weapons workers, but also for prospective nuclear chemists and physicists, mathematicians, and others who are attracted to this kind of work and may want to find a growth industry. Certainly waste management is going to be a growth industry.

The current travails of the United States and the former Soviet Union indicate some of the problems that must now be addressed. There are environmental and health problems, the cleanup challenge, and the muddled rationale for maintaining large nuclear forces. All of these problems have emerged simultaneously, as proliferation has become the dominant national or international security threat that leaders are confronting.

If the past and present are a prologue to the future, these problems will be approached piecemeal, one-at-a-time, and nationally. This will include the nonproliferation regime with its reliance on six or more export control vehicles: the Non-Proliferation Treaty (NPT), the Nuclear Suppliers' Group, COCOM (Coordinating Committee on Export Controls), the Missile Technology Control Regime, and some other national legislation. All this is ad hoc, and as one administration official said last week, these regimes are all bumping into each other as they grow; it is fairly disorganized.

While much good work can and should be done to ensure that this ad hoc, national approach goes forward and yields positive results, I think as much energy now should be devoted to devising another way. We should test the capacity for imagination to develop a grand strategy, a clear concept to stop the spread of nuclear weapons and manage the steady dismantlement of current arsenals. We need a strategy with a clear statement of goals that provides moral and political vision which can rally publics and governments to a cause. As it now stands, virtually no one understands nonproliferation policy. It is totally unglamorous and a lousy career path in the government. This will remain the case until leaders make nonproliferation a major reason for our political being, and elaborate a grand strategy.

Next, all the little steps can be fitted into a context that begins to make sense for people. In my view, two central objectives need to go into such a grand strategy. One is disarming the world of existing arsenals, and the other is stopping the development and spread of new weapons and weapons materials. These two objectives, disarmament and nonproliferation, are interdependent, even if that fact is not adequately appreciated. The objectives are formally related in Article VI of the Non-Proliferation Treaty, wherein the countries that agree not to acquire nuclear weapons do so in return for the nuclear powers' commitment to negotiate in good faith, to cease the nuclear arms race at an early date, and to achieve nuclear disarmament. This trade-off hasn't adequately been fulfilled, and that needs to be part of the strategy.

Furthermore, beyond the political linkage between disarmament and nonproliferation, there is a technical linkage that hasn't been adequately recognized. The continued production of nuclear weapons by the recognized nuclear powers makes it harder to prevent the transfer of those materials and know-how to proliferators. So disarmament and nonproliferation is not just a political issue. It is a technical and physical issue where we have to disarm and stop producing in order to minimize the chance of proliferation.

A third related component of this effort to achieve disarmament and stop proliferation is that the grand strategy for rolling back the threat of nuclear war must be global and nondiscriminatory. Much greater efforts must be made to apply the strategy to everyone equitably. It is an issue of treating like as like, rather than saying it's acceptable for our ally Japan to acquire 100 tons of plutonium, but for India to have one pound of undisclosed or unsafeguarded plutonium is a potential crime against humanity.

For any of this to happen, for any grand strategy to be devised and proclaimed, the leaders of the world must decide that preventing nuclear war is their fundamental personal priority. They

159

must insist that their advisers provide them with such a strategy. This political will and determination to confront the nuclear challenge head-on has been lacking for at least the last 45 years, I would argue.

There is, however, a small precedent for the approach that I am suggesting: the Acheson-Lilienthal proposal of 46 years ago. The essential logic and conclusions of the proposal offer a core around which to build a thoroughly modern and achievable disarmament and nonproliferation strategy. I believe the wisdom of the Acheson-Lilienthal report still stands out today. It proceeds from three basic premises. First, nuclear weapons present a qualitatively and quantitatively distinct threat to humankind—there is nothing like them. Second, there can be no fail-safe defense against these weapons. Third, there can be no monopoly of their possession, and the spread of these weapons cannot be prevented without concerted and cooperative efforts.

The Acheson-Lilienthal document then concluded, with ample justification, that the world could not simply outlaw the purely military development of atomic energy and rely solely on inspection for enforcement. It had to be much more comprehensive. Only a hands-on approach to nuclear technology would have any chance of succeeding. So the report proposed the creation of an international atomic development authority that would conduct

> all intrinsically dangerous operations in the nuclear field, with individual nations and their citizens free to conduct, under license and a minimum of inspection, all nondangerous or safe operations. When the plan is in full operation, no nation will be the legal owner of atomic weapons, of stockpiles of fissionable material or raw materials, or of the plants in which they can be produced.

Essentially, the international agency would have sovereign control over nuclear technology, licensing national, governmental, or private enterprises to perform power generation or other nuclear functions using the technologies and materials that the international agency concluded were safe.

George Perkovich

I cannot judge whether this plan seemed more idealistic when it was offered in 1946 than it does today; however, here is how the authors themselves confronted this charge of being overly idealistic 46 years ago:

> The program we propose will undoubtedly arouse skepticism when it is first considered. It did among us, but thought and discussion have converted us. It may seem too idealistic. It seems time, however, that we endeavor to bring some of our expressed ideals into being. It may seem too radical, too advanced, too much beyond human experience. All these terms apply with peculiar fitness to the atomic bomb. In considering the plan, as inevitable, doubts arise to its acceptability, one should ask oneself what are the alternatives. We have, and we find no tolerable answer.

I think we have lived through 45 years of the alternatives, and while nuclear war has been avoided throughout the Cold War, we are now, ironically, entering a time when the very reduction of the threat of global nuclear war reduces constraints and increases the probability of limited nuclear war. It becomes more feasible to contemplate launching a nuclear attack if one doesn't think it will trigger all-out exchanges. Thus, I believe it makes sense to go back and look at the insights of Acheson-Lilienthal.

There are fundamental differences between the respective situations in 1946 and 1992. Two of the differences are positive and one is negative. The first difference between these two historical episodes is that we are now at the *end* of the major powers' nuclear arms race, not the beginning. Second, the nuclear powers, including arguably the undeclared ones, do not need to produce any more weapons-grade fissile materials. These nations have as much weapons-grade fissile material as they need, and they have recognized this. This lack of need for such fissile material makes the technical challenge of controlling such production much simpler than it was when the arms race was just beginning.

The third major difference is the negative one—today there are large nuclear arsenals that are spread around the world, and there

161

are large stockpiles of fissile materials. As a corollary, and this may be the most difficult challenge, there are powerful military and business interests that will obstruct fundamental change in the way that nuclear materials are manufactured and held in the world today.

In today's context, what does international control of nuclear weapons mean? Most ambitiously, you could return to something like Acheson-Lilienthal and the idea of an international agency that actually manages all these operations. I would submit, however, that there is a spectrum of steps and procedures between what we have today and what Acheson-Lilienthal imagined, and if we moved along that spectrum we could achieve significant success.

In political science terms, the challenge is *regime building*. Can we build a comprehensive regime to manage this problem? It deserves much more serious examination in those terms than it has received. I will offer a quick heuristic model of how one would build such a regime. It is qualitatively different from the current nonproliferation regime, because the proposed approach is nondiscriminatory. It treats like as like. It views nuclear weapons—their production and deployment—as the problem, not the nuclear weapons making and production of this or that country.

I will present some of these items in a linear order, but the whole notion has to be organic, with different elements being pursued simultaneously. The first step in building an international regime to control nuclear weapons is that the United States and Russia have to agree to stop producing weapons-grade materials and to stop producing nuclear weapons—as of tomorrow, no more production. They would frame this act in terms of their movement toward fulfilling Article VI of the Non-Proliferation Treaty. In the U.S. case, this would merely be ratification of the status quo—we haven't produced highly enriched uranium since 1964, and we stopped producing plutonium in 1989. The Russians have said that they would stop all production if we agreed to a formal treaty on this matter. So far our government has refused, for reasons that are unclear.**

**The United States formally declared a cessation of production of highly enriched uranium and plutonium in July 1992.*

George Perkovich

As part of this halt in production, the United States and Russia would accept verification and safeguards on every facility. Here too, in current reports about the dismantlement of Russian nuclear weapons, there is an ironic twist: The United States does not want to monitor and verify what the Russians do with the fissile materials they are taking out of those weapons. This turns the principle of verification, upon which President Reagan and others always insisted, on its head. We don't want to insist on international accounting and verification of Russian materials because the Russians would insist that it be reciprocal. The United States doesn't want to say what it is going to do with its fissile materials because it wants to reserve the option of making new weapons with them. This obstacle must be overcome.

The second step in building the regime is for both the United States and Russia to simultaneously declare an intention to launch a comprehensive international effort to end nuclear weapons production and facilitate nuclear disarmament worldwide, and thereby fulfill Article VI of the NPT as ambitiously as the world community will allow. Elements of this have been tried rhetorically, but it has never been pushed with any significant seriousness toward the other declared nuclear powers.

One way to demonstrate that we are serious about disarmament and halting nuclear weapons production is to confront two fundamental issues that we have been avoiding. First, we need to address the question: If nuclear powers insist on preserving at some level the deterrent effect we ascribe to nuclear weapons, how can we effectively—not to mention fairly—demand that other nations forego their sovereign right to seek this deterrent effect for themselves? This is the nub of the inequity dispute that has afflicted nonproliferation over the years. It is not an idle moral issue; it is a powerful question. We won't give up our nuclear weapons because we say they have a deterring value, and yet we tell other people they can't have nuclear weapons because they don't need them. Other nations ask, If the weapons are a deterrent value for you, then why must *we* forego this? We really don't have an answer to that, except "Trust us," and that tends not to be good enough. In my opinion, one clear way to address this equality issue is to frame it slightly differently and say, "What are some security

163

guarantees that the nuclear powers can offer nonnuclear countries or undeclared nuclear powers to substitute for a nuclear deterrent?"

This whole effort of providing security guarantees will be easier if we simultaneously confront another fundamental issue that we have avoided, and that is the question of the first use of nuclear weapons. The circles in which the Foundation travels, in the sense of those people to whom we make grants, have been clear for a long time that no-first-use must be accepted. In fact, it is unconscionable and militarily nonsensical at this point and time for a nation to continue to insist that it would reserve the right to use nuclear weapons first.

This declaration of no-first-use is something that the nonnuclear countries want to hear from us. I was at a dinner recently in Washington, however, where one of the authors of an influential report on nuclear policy to the administration insisted that we should not abandon first-use and should continue to declare that we would use nuclear weapons first in a conflict. There is still a long way to go on this issue, but until the no-first-use issue is confronted head-on, little progress will be made in nonproliferation.

There is another fundamental question that has to be addressed while all this is happening, something that the intellectual community hasn't really tackled: the United States nominally insists that it must maintain a number of nuclear weapons greater than the combined number of France, Britain, and China combined (leaving Russia aside). The strategic rationale for this has not been addressed. It is just a blanket assertion. Congressman Aspin makes the assertion. The administration makes the assertion. People around the world are asking why, and there really isn't an answer.

The only answer I have heard is that politically, the American people wouldn't accept having fewer nuclear weapons than everyone else combined. This is an area that requires work, because if we are going to manage this problem and reduce arsenals worldwide, we must determine the relationship between China and the United States. For example, shall we always maintain today's proportional relationship between our arsenal and China's, or should we narrow the difference? If the difference will narrow, what is the strategically optimal ratio? Can we win Chinese nuclear reductions without accepting greater equity than we have thus far?

The third step in building an international regime to control nuclear weapons is to empower the U.N. Security Council to enforce and extend the existing international safeguard agreements that monitor and track nuclear weapons capabilities. A fourth step, and all these steps would happen nearly simultaneously, is to pursue a global cessation of weapons-grade material production, civilian and military, so that everyone in the world must stop producing weapons-grade fissile materials by the 1995 review conference of the Non-Proliferation Treaty. In effect, this isn't as grand as it sounds. It is grand, but the Indians have said they would be interested in such a halt in production if the nuclear powers agreed to stop producing new weapons. The hardest sell in stopping production of plutonium and uranium will be Japan, which has an ambitious plutonium breeder reactor program that is clearly for civilian purposes—they want to generate power with it. The only problem is that it is an economic loser. It costs more to generate power this way than any other way. They have a great deal invested in it, however, so they will resist a cutoff of plutonium production. This is a challenge that has to be met head-on.

The fifth step in building the regime is to carry out a complete inventory. This has been proposed already in the Russian-American context. The serial numbers on every nuclear weapon would be collected, an inventory on all the fissile materials would be declared, and this would be used as a baseline for tracking what is out there. The Russians are willing to do this, but the United States is not quite sure whether it wants to take this step or not.

All these steps stop short of the Acheson-Lilienthal idea of an international agency to control nuclear weapons. There are serious people who propose cutting off all nuclear production to the extent possible, and then putting the remaining production under an international authority. This has appeal, especially to Third World countries, because in some sense the international authority would subsidize some of the production. The international authority would basically be saying, "We'll provide the fuel needed for civil nuclear energy, so it doesn't need to be nationally provided." The only reason a nation would insist on a national provision of nuclear fuel is if it wanted to have a clandestine weapons program. So fuel would be provided internationally and no one would produce fissile materials nationally.

While all this management of the production side is occurring, I would argue that an additional international element needs to be included to devise alternative agendas for existing nuclear weapons expertise. This follows the Acheson-Lilienthal idea, except they didn't recognize that waste would be a problem. The waste problem was not anticipated, no one thought much about it, and it wasn't really important. Now it is turning out to be extremely important. Therefore, I would argue that an international approach to devising technologies for managing waste and cleanup should be employed, and that this provides a way to draw proliferation-sensitive individuals into constructive work. They would be paid to do waste management innovations and cleanup.

Secondly, this international approach would deploy nuclear weapons specialists to improve civilian reactor safety. There was a recent report that a civilian reactor near Saint Petersburg (formerly Leningrad) in Russia had an accident, and radioactive gas was released. There are roughly 50 such reactors in the former Soviet Union. All are extremely unsafe. As you can imagine, the Germans are very upset and worried about this. Redeploying weapons expertise to build up these reactors and design new safety features is very much in the international community's interest, and there is plenty of demand for this.

This brings us to the last question, which is about weapons. Hypothetically, we have managed the production and the fissile materials, and we have some ideas on what to do with the scientists (get them involved in the waste management and reactor safety), but all these weapons are already there. What do we do with them?

On this problem, there are a number of arms control steps that I will skip; I want to go right to the question, an extension of the Acheson-Lilienthal logic, which is, Should an internationally controlled nuclear deterrent arsenal be contemplated? In other words, should we go from the current national nuclear forces to some kind of internationally controlled arsenal, perhaps controlled by the U.N. Security Council? Such an idea does not presuppose a world government. It is similar to a republican model much like our government, where the relationship is between states. One person who has thought about this is a young political scientist at Penn, Dan Deudnoy, who speaks of it in terms of augmenting the state system with something like a check-and-balance system on the use of nuclear weapons.

The argument is logically sharp. Many of the technical details have to be worked out, although, for example, one can immediately imagine that the territory problem could be overcome by putting the nuclear weapons on submarines. There are also many command and control problems, but the basic logic is that a small internationally controlled arsenal would presumably eliminate or decisively reduce the demand for nuclear weapons among nonnuclear states. In other words, a country such as Pakistan, for example, would trade in its undeclared nuclear deterrent for a nuclear deterrent in which it has a vote. It is an international nuclear deterrent force. Or, a country that doesn't even have a nuclear weapons capability is approached and told, "You are getting the benefits of a nuclear deterrent without the cost of developing an indigenous nuclear force and violating the NPT Treaty." Many questions obviously need to be answered in pursuing this proposal, but it certainly deserves serious analysis as a future step in disarmament and nonproliferation policy.

There are, however, some precedents that make an international nuclear arsenal seem more feasible if one considers the debate in the U.N. Security Council about whether the European Community should be given a seat. Britain and France have a seat on the Security Council now. Neither of them is a great power compared, let's say, to Germany or Japan. One argument is to fudge the effect of kicking France or Britain out by having a European Community seat at the U.N. Security Council—one seat representing the interests of many states. This begins to approach the kind of sharing of decision making and power that I am talking about with an international nuclear arsenal.

A similar issue is the discussion of creating a European deterrent. If NATO becomes weak, and there is a more collective European security arrangement, would there be an EC-managed nuclear deterrent to replace the separately managed French and British nuclear forces? In any case, whether or not one goes through the rigorous analysis on an international deterrent force, I think you have to address the fundamental issues it raises. If an international arsenal isn't acceptable, then we must answer the alternative question, What security guarantees can a nuclear power provide to the nonnuclear and undeclared nuclear powers that will motivate them to forgo nuclear weapons development? These are fundamental questions that the system has not yet addressed.

In closing, let me say that national bureaucracies won't develop any of this. Political leadership at the highest level is required for a comprehensive approach to solving the nuclear problem, and those leaders will be resisted by their own bureaucracies, as plenty of experience shows. One vivid example of that dichotomy between political leadership and bureaucracies was at Reykjavík, which is an episode that is often belittled. When one looks at it, however, there was great merit to what Gorbachev and Reagan were on the verge of agreeing to, which was to abolish *all* U.S. and Soviet nuclear weapons in ballistic missiles. When they stepped out of the hall, the representatives of the various bureaucracies beat them over the head about it, and they backed off of this dramatic proposal.

I think a similar parallel was the Acheson-Lilienthal report, which showed the kind of high-powered, high-profile political leadership that is required to address this problem. If it doesn't happen at that level, it is not going to happen. I don't know where we will go to get that leadership, but it is the precondition for making all of this happen.

QUESTION: In terms of the structural tactics of trying to achieve the international control of nuclear weapons, haven't you omitted the question of the cessation of testing, both of nuclear explosions and of missiles? A cessation of testing seems to have with it the capacity to communicate some of the reassurance you are seeking, and seems now to be the major impediment.

MR. PERKOVICH: Yes, a halt in nuclear weapons testing is an absolute requirement in achieving some sort of international regime to control nuclear weapons. I was told by two administration representatives that they wanted to continue testing in perpetuity.

George Perkovich

QUESTION: How do you respond to people who argue that for 46 years we have approached this problem at the wrong end? For example, the Ukraine and Russia worry about the use of each other's weapons. They distrust each other, and each is afraid the other will try to become dominant. Therefore, until we tackle the political problem, until we try to remove the underlying tensions that so often manifest themselves in disputes, any amount of tinkering with the technical end of arms control still leaves the underlying mistrust which is so widespread. This situation was recently expressed dramatically in the Ukraine's position that yes, maybe they will destroy their nuclear weapons, but they won't give them to the Russians and let the Russians gain that much more supremacy over them.

MR. PERKOVICH: It is absolutely true that one has to be concerned about the fundamental attitudes and intentions of competing states, and the weapons often are symbols of that competition. The reverse is also true, however, insofar as the existence of the weapons and the capabilities fuels worst-case analysis and political argumentation back and forth. So, the weapons apparatus becomes a demonstration of mal-intent from the other country, which then fuels one's own hatred for the other country, and soon political intention and technical apparatuses create a spiral of action-reaction. I would argue that, in fact, working on the weapons side of the problem—which we saw in the U.S.-Soviet context—actually starts to soften the political dispute. Even at the height of the Cold War, there were agreements being negotiated to avoid nuclear war—the Crisis Intervention Center and so on. The process of negotiating these agreements, in fact, started to warm relations.

So I think you are right that we need to go to the fundamentals; however, a great deal can also be accomplished by working on the weapons side. It is also true that the antipathy between nations creates arms competition in many cases. Furthermore, I would argue that just as strong a factor in creating arms competition among nations is the vested interest of the weapons complex's internal bureaucratic establishment within each country. Over time, countries forget why they are competing with

169

each other, but they have vast bureaucracies within each country that drive this competition forward.

As an example, we were at a meeting in Washington three weeks ago, and the leaders of the two Russian nuclear weapons labs were there. They were talking about how leaders from Livermore and Los Alamos had just been to Russia two weeks before that. They were sitting at Arzamas 16, which is one of the main weapons labs, when the Russian host said to the director of Los Alamos, "Isn't it amazing that here we are. We have been building nuclear weapons all these years with the notion that perhaps we would use them on each other. You are our enemy in all of this, and now here you are, and we are cooperating."

The leader from Los Alamos, Siegfried Heckler, said, "No, you don't understand. The Russians were never our enemy. Livermore was our enemy." I think that is true. This was told to me by the Russian who then said, "In our country, too, you were never our enemy. It was Chelyabinsk 70 that was our enemy." So, I think the internal drive towards armaments is as strong as any kind of enmity between countries.

COMMENT: The opposite view, as you know, is that until Khrushchev and Kennedy began to let one another know that they could be tough, as at Vienna, but also that they were willing to bargain, you didn't get the Limited Test Ban Treaty. In the same way, until Reagan and Gorbachev began meeting and seemed to suggest the possibility of relaxation of tension, you didn't get any arms agreements between them.

QUESTION: I am impressed with your interest in developing a new regime modeled after Acheson-Lilienthal. I recall that at the time there were real questions about the nature of the regime to be created, particularly on two problems. One, how do you get this new bureaucracy, this new regime, to actually make the decisions when confronted with the tough cases? Secondly, how do you police this new regime if it makes the wrong decision? This recognizes that while a completely impartial and neatly operating regime is desirable, it is more likely to be political.

George Perkovich

MR. PERKOVICH: In some instances, it is easier now, because one can create a regime without having to create the international entity that Acheson-Lilienthal imagined. For example, we can achieve a cutoff of fissile material production internationally without a transcendent organization.

When you extrapolate from this, however, there *is* a role for some type of international entity, especially a possible international nuclear deterrent force. There are all kinds of operational questions that would have to be addressed, and I certainly don't have the answers. My notion would be to continue working and call upon more experienced people than I to try to flesh out the details. It is a problem that obviously doesn't go away.

It is not clear that these problems are greater or more problematic than the current status quo. It is a question of, does the unattainability of perfection keep you from trying something that's good? It is a tough call.

QUESTION: A recent speaker made an interesting comment to the effect that he could see the possibility of a nonproliferation program working, but this would apply only to those who chose to join the club. Various rogue nations would still be on their own. His point was that the ease of making a nuclear weapon is such that there is no secret to how you do it, and that clearly it could be done by a number of nations who wouldn't choose to join the group. The extreme problem, as he saw it, was how to handle these people who are not members of a nonproliferation grouping or regime. In other words, if any country declares its intention to join a nonproliferation group, you have the beginning of a nucleus, but what about those that don't join?

MR. PERKOVICH: Those nations choosing not to join would not be an abstract number; it is a known number. You know that France and China will join, while Pakistan and India would be among the small number who wouldn't join. I think that if international leaders, beginning with our own, say that nonproliferation is a big deal and they are going on a mission to work on this problem, then you can take care of India and Pakistan this way.

North Korea may be coming into line now, although it isn't clear. The other option in all this is the "stick," which is a conventional preemptive strike. If the international community weighs in heavily and does some of the things I talked about within the context of a regime that is widely recognized to be equitable and in everyone's interest, then we have a situation similar to that of Iraq taking over Kuwait. Getting an international consensus to strike against a rogue actor in this circumstance wouldn't be insurmountable, actually, because the renegade action would be so outrageous that the rest of the community could be mobilized. At that point, the rogue nation is isolated. In the case of North Korea, for example, they are already isolated. Then the issue is, Do you launch a conventional preemptive strike against their nuclear facilities? It is an option, but one which can and should be avoided.

The reason North Korea isn't such a problem is that it has an indigenous production capacity—it has a huge detectable apparatus to make a nuclear weapon. The harder problem is imaging a subnational organization or a terrorist group that doesn't make their own weapon but somehow buys one. In that case, what are your options? You probably don't know where the terrorists are located, and even if the location of the terrorists is known, there is not a large area that can be bombed to destroy their nuclear capacity. This is a harder case, and my response to it is that we can't do anything about it today, either. So this isn't an argument against an international regime. If it is a subnational rogue, we are no worse off with an international regime than we are today without one.

QUESTION: I'm confused about the role of civil nuclear power within your regime. I thought I understood it until you mentioned the problem associated with the Japanese breeder reactor program.

MR. PERKOVICH: On civil nuclear power the issue is that one would proscribe—eliminate—fuel cycles that rely on weapons-grade material. Plutonium fuel cycles would be proscribed, because this fuel is inherently susceptible to weapons proliferation and in any case is too uneconomic to be competitive until the end of the next century, if then.

QUESTION: I don't understand nuclear power without the production of plutonium.

MR. PERKOVICH: You use uranium. There would be no plutonium reprocessing, so those facilities would be shut down. A once-through fuel cycle with uranium would be used, and then there would be agreement on treating the waste in ways that can be verified and monitored so that no one could then divert the waste to extract plutonium from it. The waste problem isn't as great if reprocessing facilities have already been proscribed.

QUESTION: I don't understand the distinction. The waste now contains plutonium and it also contains the long-lived transuranic elements. It also contains massive amounts of potential energy-producing material, which under your regime would be discarded, I gather.

MR. PERKOVICH: Yes, because today and in the foreseeable future, it is economically inefficient to reprocess that waste to use it for fuel. It is much more efficient to continue burning uranium once through without reprocessing the waste. So you just ratify that.

COMMENT: When you say foreseeable future, you are talking about 30 or 40 years. It seems to me that our future should be longer than that.

MR. PERKOVICH: I would choose to invest in innovation that avoids relying on plutonium rather than investing in a future that has plutonium transiting all around the world. I would take the gamble that such research and development will succeed. I would be willing to take whatever risk associated with this gamble, which would preclude Japan from getting the 100 tons of plutonium it is scheduled now to receive, rather than buying into a plutonium economy. The studies I have seen say that the once-through uranium cycle can go for longer than four decades when you start using the highly enriched uranium that is coming out of retired weapons.

QUESTION: With respect to the civilian use of nuclear energy, and given the need for energy that exists in the underdeveloped areas of the world, if we really go forward with a worldwide program to rely upon once-through uranium based on today's technology, how much of a load would it take away from weapons production? In other words, you would not use any of that material except for the purpose of civilian energy. I know the number of weapons that exists is tremendous. I don't know how much it represents in total tons of plutonium, but it is a great deal. If you are never going to replace that and are going to use all of the uranium in the world for the purpose of civilian power and the good of the world, does this in effect offer a position where there is no more raw material left to make weapons eventually?

MR. PERKOVICH: I don't know about eventually. The fissile materials in weapons can last as long as plutonium lasts, which is many millennia, so if you were going to retain an arsenal, you could just recycle and move it around, which is in essence what we are going to do now that the Rocky Flats plant in Colorado is closed.

COMMENT: If we destroy that plutonium and those weapons one way or another, it is not easy to go back into that business if you are using the uranium for other purposes all over the world. It seems to me that we are getting away from the idea of the tremendous economic means of producing energy for electricity, which is essential to improving the well-being of all the citizens of the world. Without it, these countries are going to stay the way they are now.

MR. PERKOVICH: I'm not so sure how economic it is to use nuclear power if you start factoring in the waste and the cost of decommissioning.

COMMENT: If you think of the money that is spent on weapons, however, it certainly *is* economic. We simply don't have any alternatives that will supply the energy needs of the world.

George Perkovich

MR. PERKOVICH: The other side of the Foundation works a great deal on energy policy within the environmental program, and I am told there are a number of alternatives to nuclear power. If you take away the subsidies to nuclear power and factor in the waste costs, which are externalized, it isn't as attractive as it seems. This is why developed and developing countries alike are moving away from nuclear power.

COMMENT: I think if you begin looking at the fossil fuels as our means, we certainly have enough coal in this country to last 500 years at the current consumption rate. We know, however, that fossil fuels create a great deal of pollution. Furthermore, there is a finite reserve of fossil fuels, and it seems to me that there ought to be more push in the domestic area.

NARRATOR: Mr. Perkovich has proven today that he is someone who initiates and puts forward ideas that have a chance to bring about a better future. We have had an excellent example of what can be accomplished when someone has the courage and insight to challenge us to rethink prior assumptions and to consider assumptions that might take their place. Thank you very much.